Social Ethics

DISCARDED
From Nashville Public Library

Social Ethics

A Student's Guide

Jenny Teichman

First published 1996
Reprinted 1999

Blackwell Publishers Ltd
108 Cowley Road
Oxford OX4 1JF
UK

Blackwell Publishers Inc.
350 Main Street
Malden, Massachusetts 02148
USA

British Library Cataloguing in Publication Data

A CIP catalogue record for this book is available from the British Library.

Library of Congress Cataloging-in-Publication Data

Teichman, Jenny.
    Social ethics: a student's guide/Jenny Teichman.
        p. cm.
    Includes bibliographical references and index.
    ISBN 0–631–19608–0 (hbk.:alk. paper). — ISBN 0–631–19609–9 (pbk.:alk. paper)
        1. Social ethics.   I. Title.
    HM216.T35   1996
    170 – dc20   96-6455
                                                                              CIP

Typeset in 11.5 on 13.5 pt Bembo
By Best-set Typesetter Ltd., Hong Kong

This book is printed on acid-free paper

Contents

Contents

Preface

This book gives a reasoned defence of the humanistic ethical codes which the twentieth century has inherited from a number of different sources. It is opposed to the 'new moralities' first propounded in popular economic and philosophical primers and then taken up by politicians and journalists. The supporters of the 'new moralities' accept peculiar slogans (like 'greed is good') and invent peculiar new terms of abuse (like 'speciesism'). One very influential 'new morality' recommends that we give up the idea that human beings have any natural rights or any special worth.

The 'new moralities' are not humanistic except in the narrow sense of that word in which humanism simply means atheism. Humanism in the wider sense is based on a fundamental respect for human life. The broad intuitive appeal of this larger humanism means that its fundamental premises are accepted by many people in many nations. It is compatible with religious belief and also with unbelief. Its sources include the great monotheistic religions, the ideas and idealism generated by the American and French revolutions, the aspirations made manifest at the founding of the League of Nations and the United Nations Organization, and the teachings of great thinkers such as Locke, Condorcet, Kant, M. K. Gandhi and E. F. Schumacher.

The first part of this book discusses, and rejects, three well-known theories about the nature of moral judgement and goes on to defend the premise that human life is sacred in a secular sense. The second part argues that all reasonable moral judgements and any reasonable moral philosophy must value human life and accept the importance of universal human rights. The third part examines controversial issues about life and death. The fourth part is concerned with the ideological issues of feminism and anti-feminism, freedom of thought and expression, economic liberty, and ecology.

There are two appendices. One contains excerpts from constitutional documents illustrating the important role, in Western political thought, of the concept of universal human rights; the other briefly traces the course of an ongoing controversy about euthanasia in Australia.

There is a glossary explaining the meanings of a number of words that might be unfamiliar to some readers, and a bibliography listing the books and articles directly or indirectly referred to in the main text.

Acknowledgements

I am very much indebted to David Braine, of the University of Aberdeen, for allowing me to borrow some of his ideas; to Cora Diamond, of the University of Virginia, for permission to make use of her essay on 'Eating Meat and Eating People'; to Dr James Gilbert MRCP, of the Exeter and District Hospice, for permission to quote from his paper 'Palliative Care'; and to the Rev. Dr J. F. Searle, consultant anaesthesiologist at the Royal Devon and Exeter Hospital and Anglican priest, for permission to quote from his paper 'Euthanasia: the Intensive Care Unit'. I would also like to thank Susan Haack, of the University of Miami, for material borrowed from her paper 'Knowledge and Propaganda'; Dr Brian Pollard, of Sydney, for material borrowed from his article about Holland; and my cousin-in-law Dr Philip Tiernan, of Melbourne, for sending me much interesting information on recent changes in Australian law.

The author and publishers wish to thank the following for permission to use copyright material:

The Spectator for an extract from an article by Peter Singer in *The Spectator*, 16 Sept. 1995.

Every effort has been made to trace all the copyright holders, but if any have been inadvertently overlooked the publishers will be pleased to make the necessary arrangement at the first opportunity.

PART ONE

Ethical Bedrock

CHAPTER ONE

Morality and Humanity

'Ways of thinking are ways of existing.'

Iris Murdoch, *Metaphysics as a Guide to Morals*

Ethics, or moral philosophy, aims to explain the nature of good and evil. It is important because whether we like it or not the human world is dominated by ideas about right and wrong and good and bad. Most ordinary conversation consists of value judgements. Every day millions of people gossip about the awful things the neighbours have done or are suspected of having done. Every day people pass judgement on politicians and other public figures. Every day the characters depicted in books and films and TV programmes are evaluated by ordinary folk all over the world.

Moral philosophy is important for the further reason that action is important and the way people act is influenced by what they believe about good and evil. It used to be thought that ethical theories do not affect behaviour. But there is no basis for this view, which indeed is shown to be false by ordinary observation. Different theories make people behave in different ways. Thus consequentialists [see Glossary] are more likely than deontologists to praise or punish actions because of their results; rights theorists have a tendency to egalitarian behaviour; and cultural relativists are more likely than non-relativists to 'go with the swim'.

The intention of this book is to provide an alternative to some currently fashionable approaches to ethical issues.

One motive for providing an alternative is that philosophical

3

orthodoxy numbs the minds of students. Students who are made to concentrate on theories that happen to be fashionable at the time don't get enough mental exercise; and, as Bertrand Russell said, swimming against the tide is the best exercise there is.

But the main reason for defending what is nowadays an unorthodox ethical viewpoint – unorthodox in the academies, that is – is that the orthodox notions currently accepted as bedrock by many philosophy teachers imply conclusions which conflict with the kind of humane attitudes that have led individuals and societies out of barbarism into civilization. That implication was probably not intended by all the teachers who espouse those notions. Nevertheless it is no bad thing if philosophers who can see the implications should draw attention to them.

The dogmas supported, or presupposed, by some very popular textbooks on moral philosophy include the following:

1 The idea that human life as such is not worthy of special respect.

2 The idea that happiness and misery, pleasure and pain, are more important than life itself.

3 The idea that only people who have a certain degree of intelligence and self-awareness have any right to life; according to this view infants, for example, must be denied a natural right to life.

4 The idea that in order to have needs and wants and rights a being must first have the concepts of, or the words for, *need, want, right.*

5 The idea that moral theory should conform as much as possible to whatever happens to be social practice at the time.

These five dogmas are fundamentally at odds with the belief that human life has intrinsic value and with the principle that human beings as such have rights. So it is not surprising that when teachers and students accept them they find themselves pushed by logic into defending a number of dubious practical proposals. Thus it is sometimes argued, from dogma five, above, that if certain practices (such as 'involuntary' euthanasia) have already been accepted by our society anyway, they 'can't really be wrong', or, conversely, that primitive societies, which are 'closer to nature', have always adopted those practices, so again 'they can't be wrong'.

We can agree with the logic of the professors but that does not mean that we have to accept the dogmas which their reasoning starts from. Illogical thinking is not good thinking, of course, but logical reasoning which starts from false premises is no good either.

In the real world there are societies whose morals and politics are explicitly or implicitly based on the theory that human life as such is of no special value. These societies are not nice places in which to live. They don't mind treating some people – for example, Jews or the bourgeoisie or Bosnians or members of noble families – as vermin to be killed or enslaved. The philosophy professor Jonathan Glover states that his attempts to show that 'conventional moral views about killing' are unsatisfactory (he means the 'conventional' view that killing innocent people is bad) 'in no way give support' to the attitudes of those who performed medical experiments on people in Auschwitz. This seems a very reckless statement. There is a straightforward logical connection between the proposition that human life has no special value and the proposition that its value, if any, is merely instrumental. There is an obvious logical connection between that second proposition and the proposition that treating individual human beings as experimental animals is, or could be, a legitimate scientific procedure. Now, if a scientist believes that a certain procedure is legitimate there is every reason, other things being equal, to suppose that if he thinks it fruitful he will either carry it out himself one day, or will give moral support to those of his fellow scientists who do.

The intuition that one's own life, and the lives of those one loves, are worthy of respect, is surely to be found in all the

5

families and races and nations of the world. It is very natural, after all, that most human beings should be attracted to the idea that human life is intrinsically valuable! Still, students and others are often told by philosophy teachers in the West that their central moral intuition, the value they instinctively place on human life, is based on nothing better than sentimentalism, and 'speciesism', and outmoded religious notions.

However, academic attacks on 'speciesism' and sentimentality and religion are all beside the point, because the widespread intuitions about the value of human life can be defended by reason.

Every philosophy has bedrock propositions which are not questioned. This has to be so, otherwise philosophical reasoning would be circular. But that does not mean that all possible bedrocks are equally rational. For an ethical bedrock to be rational it must be suitable for the human condition, it must be humane, it must not take the social malfunctions caused by wars and extreme poverty and brutal colonization as standards to imitate, and it must not have real-world implications which would be unwelcome, when recognized (perhaps too late!), even to those who rest their faith on it.

CHAPTER TWO

Egoism, Relativism, Consequentialism

'I reject all these foreign isms . . .'

F. D. Roosevelt

The account of moral philosophy as aimed at discovering the nature of good and evil would be accepted by most philosophers but the theories they produce are of course quite various. This chapter examines three currently popular views or 'isms'.

Egoism

Egoism can be defined as either practical or theoretical. Practical egoism consists in behaviour characterized by systematic selfishness, theoretical egoism is a theory which bases morality on self-interest. Similarly altruism, the opposite of egoism, is also either practical or theoretical. Practical altruism consists of behaviour characterized by systematic unselfishness, theoretical altrusim is a theory which bases morality entirely or largely on the interests of others. In what follows I shall be discussing theoretical egoism.

Theoretical egoism comprises four distinct ideas, or interpretations, which are not always kept separate.

On the first interpretation egoism is a theory about human nature. It is the theory that all human beings are always motivated by selfishness and that seemingly unselfish actions are really selfish actions in disguise.

7

Ethical Bedrock

Now, an apparent desire to help another person *might* disguise a selfish motive, but there is no reason to suppose that is always the case. The study of animal behaviour, including human behaviour, shows that altruism as well as egoism is part of the behavioural repertoire of all gregarious creatures and especially mammals. Secondly, the hypothesis of 'the selfish gene' indicates that all animals act selflessly on occasion, they are capable of altruism in a literal sense of that word. It is genes, not individual animals, that behave in a purely selfish manner.

Another interpretation rests on the premise that one's desire to help others is always really selfish because the desire itself must belong to the desirer. But this involves a simple misunderstanding. It muddles up *having* a desire with the *content* of a desire. Ownership and content are two separate things and it is the content, not the ownership, of the desire which determines whether it is selfish or altrusitic.

Yet another interpretation consists in the dogma that selfishness is more rational than unelfishness. The free-market economists of the Austrian School hold that self-interest is the only motive that can effectively produce a healthy and wealthy society; some of their arguments are examined in chapter 13. Amongst philosophy teachers the common assumption that egoism is rational is exemplified in the work of a North American professor, David Gauthier, and less directly in a book by Thomas Nagel. The title of Nagel's book, *The Possibility of Altruism*, somehow conveys the impression that altruism is unnatural and almost but not quite impossible.

Can one prove that egoism is more rational than altruism? Egoism tends to benefit oneself, of course. Is that a proof? No, because we cannot prove that benefiting oneself is more rational than not without assuming the point to be proved. There is, indeed, a tendency among philosophy professors to *presuppose* that egoism is rational, to take this proposition as axiomatic; but it is open for anyone who wants to, to adopt the opposite premise, namely, that altruism is more rational than egoism. Perhaps that can't be proved either, but as an axiom it is just as good as the other one. The egoist is rational according to his own axiom, and the altruist is rational according to his (or more likely hers).

The fourth interpretation of theoretical egoism is based on the philosophy of Friedrich Nietzsche. It is the view that, whether or not egoism is common or uncommon, natural or unnatural, it *ought* to be adopted. Nietzsche claimed that superior human beings ought to adopt egoism in order to improve the human race. If superior individuals acted in a fully egoistic manner the inferior specimens of humanity would disappear, making way for a Nietzschean *Übermensch* (superman).

However, the idea that human beings can be classified as inferior and superior doesn't make sense unless you are *evaluating* them. If you are evaluating muscles then boxers are superior people. It would be possible to evaluate your fellow citizens in economic terms, giving high marks to millionaires and low marks to itinerants. If you are evaluating things from a moral point of view you might well decide that selfless behaviour is a mark of superiority. Classifying people as superior or inferior because they are strong or weak (mentally or physically) is arbitrary and un-natural. The man in the wheelchair might be a brilliant astronomer and the class dunce might one day save you from drowning. We need also to remember just what kinds of people actually act on the principle that some groups of human beings are essentially inferior to the rest of us. The conscious and unconscious follow-ers of Nietzsche, the men who put his principles into practice, are dictators and war criminals.

Relativism

Cultural relativists hold that what is right or wrong, good or bad, depends entirely on the society you live in. They notice that different societies have different codes of behaviour and then infer that morality as such is 'relative to', and created by, particu-lar societies. Thus an anthropological fact is thought to entail a conclusion about the nature of good and evil. It is said, then, that there is no right or wrong above or beyond social norms and no way in which different social norms can be objectively compared or ranked. You should not judge another community by the rules which govern your own for to do that is to engage in cultural imperialism. It is safest not to judge anyone at all because even a citizen of your own country might not share your opinions or the opinions of your community.

But aren't there some rules which every society accepts, which every rational person accepts? Well, most communities have rules which protect property (or the property of rich people) and virtually all have rules against the random killing of human beings. Perhaps the widest variations occur in the area of sexual morality and for that reason relativists almost always mention sexual matters as evidence in favour of their theories. Thus the philosophy professor J. L. Mackie places weight on the fact that polygamy is forbidden in some countries and permitted in others. Variation between the customs of different societies is, however, consistent with non-relativism, and for two reasons. First, if two societies are radically different it is logically possible that one is a bad and evil society and the other is not. Secondly, it is possible for two different ways of solving a problem to be equally good while some third or fourth method is clearly bad. It is an objective fact that there can be more than one way to make a nutritious soup and it is also an objective fact that soups made from rotten ingredients are nutritionally not much good.

Different societies not only have different customs, they can also have different philosophical beliefs about the nature of morality. In this area the beliefs of traditional societies tend to be strongly anti-relativist. Traditional societies believe that what is right or wrong, good or bad, is a matter of objective fact. They hold that what is good (or bad) in one society must be good (or bad) in all societies and therefore that some societies are themselves good (or bad). Traditional communities have no difficulty in accepting the idea that the social and legal arrangements of foreign nations are worse (or better) than their own. On the other hand cultural and moral relativism is one of the principal orthodoxies of contemporary Western academic thought.

Although conscientious relativists try hard not to judge other people and other societies they find it rather difficult to stick to their principles. They can get quite excited about moral issues; for instance, relativistic thinkers are usually very hostile towards racism and elitism. How is this to be explained?

As noted above we live in a world of value. Everyone evaluates actions, friends, enemies, colleagues, jokes, books, TV programmes, music, videos and so on. Evaluation is a human necessity. But evaluation as such presupposes objective standards because if you relativize a value judgement you cancel it. The following examples show how explicitly relativized value judgements are self-cancelling:

'The activities of the Ku Klux Klan are cruel and unjust – but only of course from the point of view of black people.'

'Racism should always be condemned – except of course in societies where it is accepted.'

The qualifications ('but only' and 'except') effectively negate these judgements. Now, even the staunchest philosophical relativists find it goes against the grain to make self-cancelling evaluations and for this reason they sometimes allow a short time gap to elapse between judgement and disclaimer. But while time gaps might disguise the self-cancellations of relativistic judgements they cannot abolish them.

Moral criticism of society itself is not consistent with relativism. Yet in the real world, society itself, and social practices, are more subject to evaluation than almost anything else! Ordinary folk criticize tourists and foreigners and strange religions and unfamiliar political systems while sophisticated reformers, such as members of Amnesty International or The Howard League for Penal Reform, campaign to change the laws and customs of their own (and other) countries.

One relativistic response here is to argue that 'bad' societies are not really bad, just guilty of inconsistency. Racists, it's argued, really know that their racist theories are untenable and unscientific, tyrants know that locking people up without fair trial is irrational.

If it is true (which seems doubtful) that tyrants and racists are guilty only of inconsistency then they perpetrate, not moral crimes or sins, but intellectual errors. On the relativist view it turns out that Amnesty International is really a Logic School! It seems to me, moreover, that an inconsistent tyranny would be easier to live with than a consistent one. Sporadic inconsistent tyranny is not necessarily worse than the efficient consistent variety. Then again, if all value is relative to a society there is no reason to say that logical consistency as such is better than racism or tyranny; it all depends on the viewpoint of the society concerned.

Finally, it is very probable that every social order contains some inconsistencies. It is obvious that an ethical relativist cannot make judgements about different inconsistencies. Here as elsewhere he cannot draw objective distinctions between good and bad.

Science is taken by relativists as a paradigm of objective enquiry and as essentially different from ethics. Against this it should be noted that science itself rests on value judgements. Truth, coherence, rationality and usefulness are values which scientists believe in, explicitly or implicitly. A dilemma follows. Either truth and rationality are only relative and what is true or rational in one era might be false or irrational in another — for instance, the belief that the sun goes around the earth will be literally true at one time and literally false later. This alternative seems very improbable. Or the values of science are objective and universal, in which case it follows that values *can* be objective and universal.

Some modern French authors believe that scientific truth itself is merely relative. They are 'global' relativists. Their views have been adopted by a considerable number of British and American academics who have not been trained in philosophy or science, academics working in the fields of English Literature and Modern Languages, for example.

It is not too difficult to show that global relativism is self-refuting. If any belief is as true as any other then the belief that relativism is false is as true as any other. If everything is relative then the relative is relative too. On the other hand, if 'P is true only in Culture C' is not objectively true for all P and all C then our relativism is no longer global and global relativism turns out to be false.

If global relativism is rejected then the ethical relativist has to explain how he draws a line between the relative and the objective, between science and ethics. He has to explain why he thinks objective value is possible in one sphere and not possible in another. He cannot claim that ethics contains a logical inconsistency because there is no such inconsistency. The only 'inconsistencies' are anthropological. Now, the anthropological fact of difference in beliefs is not formally inconsistent with the possibility of objectivity in ethics, any more than the historical fact of difference in beliefs about the solar system is inconsistent with the objective truth of whatever it is that *is* true about the sun and the planets.

It can be shown that global relativism leads to epistemological solipsism and cultural relativism leads to ethical solipsism [see Glossary]. Suppose a particular society consists of two people. Then A's (relativistic) ground for believing that Q is false (or wrong) is that B believes Q is false (or wrong). But B's belief must rest on A's belief! Hence A's belief ultimately rests on his own belief and the same is the case for B. In a society of more than two people the arithmetic is more complicated but the conclusion is the same; since each person depends for his belief on the others and the others depend (in part) on him, it turns out that each person is in the end depending only on himself.

If relativism is false does that mean that there are some actions which are right in all possible circumstances? Not at all. Circumstances can alter cases. If relativism is false all that follows is that there can be objective reasons for judging some actions and states of affairs to be better (or worse) than others. As we noticed earlier, it is an objective fact that there can be more than one way

13

to make a nutritious soup and it is also an objective fact that soups made from rotten ingredients are nutritionally not much good.

Virtually all theories in moral philosophy (except of course for relativism and egoism) assume that there are objective rational foundations from which it is possible to derive judgements about what acts and states of affairs are better or worse than others. One famous, and still popular, theory is utilitarianism.

Utilitarianism and Consequentialism

Utilitarians hold that all actions and states of affairs should be judged by their results. The theory takes several forms. In Jeremy Bentham's original version pleasure is the only possible good result and pain the only bad one. In J. S. Mill's version happiness and unhappiness, rather than pleasure and pain, are the bedrock good and evil. Mill's principle states:

> Always act so as to produce the greatest possible happiness for the greatest possible number of people.

According to ideal utilitarianism (a twentieth-century development) pleasure and happiness are merely two of several types of result which ought to be aimed at. Loyal friendship, freedom, and artistic merit are some of the additional aims recommended by ideal utilitarians.

Utilitarianism can be classified as relating either to acts or to rules. Act-utilitarianism states that we ought to calculate, then judge, the probable consequences of every single actual or proposed action, whereas rule-utilitarianism claims that we should predict, then judge, the outcomes of actual or possible rules and laws.

A single name is needed for the different varieties of utilitarianism. Let us use the label 'consequentialism'. This word was coined in 1957 by Elizabeth Anscombe and is more or less self-explanatory.

It is interesting to note that the thinking of many educated individuals in the West is simultaneously relativistic and consequentialist. This is a self-contradictory stance because consequentialism holds that actions (or rules) should be judged according to results quite independently of which society they occur in.

Consequentialism, like relativism, is a good example of a theory which is dead but won't lie down. It has been repeatedly refuted but there are still significant numbers of philosophy professors who believe in it. Since most of the readers of this book will already know that consequentialism and utilitarianism have many flaws, I will simply remind them of the main defects.

1   Consequentialism cannot be put into practice because short-term consequences can't be predicted with certainty and long-term consequences cannot be predicted at all. (How long is long-term? It is infinitely or indefinitely long.)

2   There is no such thing as a 'utility calculus'. In other words it is impossible to weigh one person's happiness or pleasure against another's and impossible to weigh one's own present happiness against one's future potential happiness.

3   Attempts to put consequentialism into practice would sacrifice the rights of individuals, and of minorities, to the happiness of majorities.

4   The 'best results' principle allows rulers to decide what kinds of results are more important than others. This leads first to a 'bread and circuses' view of the principles of government and then to corruption. It is only too easy for politicians to concentrate on helping themselves and their followers to as many goods as possible while ignoring everyone else.

5   Consequentialism entails contempt for justice. Whenever an unjust rule or an individual act of injustice is thought likely to create better results (e.g., more happiness) than justice, then that act or rule becomes morally obligatory.

Consequentialism is not a bedrock, it is a quagmire.

CHAPTER THREE

Ethical Bedrock

'There [is] nothing more evident than that creatures of the same species should also be equal amongst one another.'

John Locke, *An Essay Concerning the True Original Extent and End of Civil Government*

Bedrock Principles

All moral philosophy has to start from notions which are taken as basic or bedrock. It is sometimes said that these foundational notions cannot be defended. Optimists take their basic principles to be self-evident like the axioms of geometry while pessimists suspect that bedrock premises are the result of arbitrary, subjective or 'existential' choice. In my view it is possible to defend the genuine bedrock of ethics.

Different philosophies rest on different premises. Consequentialism takes happiness or pleasure or, more generally, beneficial results, as basic. Other theories try to derive moral rules from the concept of rights. For deontologists the foundation of morality has to do with duty. Some religious thinkers believe that moral judgements must rest on the authority of scripture. Some popular scientific authors say that the most important codes of behaviour are the result of evolution and the survival of the fittest but we will have to ignore this view because the only rule it can provide for deciding between alternative options is: 'follow the crowd'.

What are the true bedrock principles on which to base moral philosophy? Here we ought to ask: What is morality for? Never

17

mind where it comes from; what is its point? Why do we have such a thing?

The short answer is: Because it is needed, we can't do without it. This draws attention to its most significant dimension. Morality does not exist primarily for the sake of the cows and the frogs and the dolphins – it answers a *human* need.

I shall argue in this chapter that there are two bedrock principles which most people believe in, in their heart of hearts. These principles have perhaps gone out of fashion to some extent, as the result of the teachings of certain philosophy professors. Nevertheless their intuitive appeal remains very strong.

The first bedrock principle is that human life is intrinsically valuable, that it is sacred in either a religious or a secular sense (or both). The second is that human beings have natural rights.

These ideas are appealing for many reasons. If we accept them we will not feel obliged to 'follow the herd'. We will not feel obliged to ignore the distinction between civilization and barbarism. We will not have to depend on armchair speculation and ivory-tower philosophies. We will be able to take science, and history, and common sense into account in our thinking. Finally, we will not end up with theories that override widespread human intuitions.

Sanctity and Intrinsic Value

Contemporary consequentialist philosophers reject the idea that human life has intrinsic value and (more vehemently) the proposition that human life is sacred in any sense. The German author, Helga Kuhse, for example, has written many articles, and a big book, and in all of these she attacks the sanctity of human life.

Philosophers reject the idea that human life is sacred mainly because they believe that sanctity is a superstitious and outmoded concept. They reason that nothing can be holy, nothing can be sacred, because there are no gods. But sacred can simply mean

18

inviolable, indefeasible, to be protected, to be safeguarded. It is easy to produce many examples of this sense of the word –

1   When Horace spoke of Homer as a sacred poet he might have meant that Homer was godlike but not that he was actually a god. Nor did Horace believe that Homer was a priest or that he spoke only of holy things.

2   Cervantes: 'history is a sacred thing in that it contains the truth'.

3   Walt Whitman: 'if anything is sacred the human body is sacred'.

4   In 1926 the editor of *The Manchester Guardian* wrote 'comment is free but facts are sacred'.

5   In international law 'the persons of ambassadors shall be held sacred'.

Secular sacredness is sometimes symbolic and sometimes rests on considerations of utility. Americans regard their flag as sacred not as a piece of coloured cloth but as a symbol of their national ideals. The persons of ambassadors, on the other hand, are treated as sacred because it is useful, indeed vitally necessary, to protect individuals whose task it is to negotiate arrangements between nations. Yet neither the value of symbols nor utility itself will fully explain the secular meaning of sanctity. The primary notion of the sacred is that there are things which should be protected in all or most circumstances and for their own sakes, things which are both intrinsically valuable and highly valuable.

Some philosophy teachers deny that there is any such thing as intrinsic value. This must be due to some kind of confusion – perhaps a confusion between intrinsic value and ultimate value – because *intrinsically valuable* is simply the opposite of *valuable as a means*. If nothing had intrinsic value the things which are valuable as means would form an infinite regress of means to means to means . . .

Ethical Bedrock

In any case virtually all philosophy teachers, no matter what they say, in fact assume that some things have intrinsic positive or negative value. Utilitarians regard happiness or pleasure as intrinsically good, consequentialists believe that only consequences can have (intrinsic) value. G. E. Moore stated that friendship and art appreciation are both intrinsically good. In his book *Causing Deaths and Saving Lives* Jonathan Glover argues that personal autonomy is good because paternalism is bad, and paternalism is bad, he seems to say, because people do not like it. However if autonomy isn't good in the first place then what people like is neither here nor there; Glover's reasoning is circular. What he really believes, probably, and hence what he ought to have said, is that paternalism is intrinsically bad. (Whether that is true is another question.)

Moral philosophy cannot do without the concept of the intrinsically good. How, though, do we know or discover which things are intrinsically good (or intrinsically bad)? How do we know that human life has intrinsic value? We know it from the following considerations:

1. Almost always people want to live, happy or not, and in this way they tell us that they hold life itself to have greater value than particular states of mind or body. No doubt life-preserving behaviour is often instinctive but that does not mean that it is unreasonable. On the contrary it is unreasonable to construct a theory of value which ignores the very things that real people value. People everywhere value their own lives and the lives of their loved ones more highly than anything else on Earth.

Utilitarianism is founded on the premise that everyone desires happiness above all else but the ordinary behaviour of ordinary people shows that premise to be false.

2. It is sometimes argued that a human life only has intrinsic value if it is a life worth living. What kind of life is worth living is usually left rather vague, philosophy teachers preferring to make claims about what lives are not worth living. It is said, for example, that lives not worth living include lives of physical hardship and suffering, lives full of serious depression and sadness,

and lives in coma. But lives in captivity, lives of sadness and illness, lives with perpetual shortages of food, are judged worth living, more often than not, *by those who actually live them.* People everywhere show by their behaviour that they think even sad and deprived lives are worth living.

3. The utilitarian premise that only states of mind (such as pleasure or happiness) have any intrinsic value, puts the cart before the horse. For how can the states and conditions of a being have intrinsic value if the being itself does not? How could states of human beings have value if human beings do not? The states and qualities of a knife (say), or of any tool or machine, have only instrumental, non-intrinsic, value because knives and machines themselves are merely instruments. Conversely if we consider something that might plausibly be said to have intrinsic value – a painting by Leonardo da Vinci for example – then it makes sense to say that its qualities too are intrinsically valuable.

4. If human life has no intrinsic value how can human beings give value to other things? How could something of secondary value understand or create any primary values?

5. As we have already noticed, societies whose morals and politics are explicitly or implicitly based on the theory that human life has no intrinsic value act quite consistently when they treat some people – for example, Jews or the bourgeoisie or Bosnians or members of noble families – as vermin to be killed or enslaved.

6. If there is a value scale at all on this earth and human life is not at the top of that scale then what could be at the top?

Does the fact that suicides occur prove that people in general think life has no intrinsic value? Surely not. It does not even show that those who commit suicide believe that. It is perfectly possible to destroy something you value; such destruction is natural to those in a state of despair.

There is further discussion of intrinsic value and 'quality of life' in chapters 7 and 8, meanwhile let us turn to our other bedrock principle, the premise that human beings have natural rights.

Ethical Bedrock

Universal Human Rights

Consequentialism originated in the late eighteenth century in the work of Jeremy Bentham, the utilitarian, while full-blown theories about natural rights are just a little older. From the very beginning many proponents of the two viewpoints regarded them as diametrically opposed. The idea of universal human rights, or natural rights, was the fundamental concept underlying and inspiring the American and French revolutions and as such was attacked by Bentham himself. Bentham described the French Declaration of Rights (1789) as a collection of 'anarchical fallacies' and all talk of natural rights as 'nonsense upon stilts'.

Modern consequentialists accept the idea of rights but redefine it. They allow a place in their thinking to the concept but the place is secondary and derivative. Rights, they say, like duty and the virtues, should be understood as notions the acceptance of which tends to increase general happiness or other good ends. Rights are not absolute, they are never natural, and they cannot, and should not, be made universal.

In contemporary Western philosophy consequentialism is popular mainly in Britain and Australia. In the United States, on the other hand, many moral philosophers take the concepts of individual natural rights as a bedrock notion which is sometimes combined with a kind of consequentialism. Michael Tooley's *A Defence of Abortion* (Oxford, 1983) is a manifestation of this combination. It would seem that the reason for the difference between British and American moral philosophy is in part a matter of national history.

There are different kinds of rights: customary rights, legal rights, civil rights, and natural, or human, rights.

Customary rights need no state to uphold them. They rest on implicit understandings and on trust. In some traditional societies ancestral property rights depend ultimately on village memory. Children often appeal to their customary rights, for example like this: 'You can't sit in that chair, I always sit there!' And this: 'It's my turn on the swing!' And this: 'Teacher lent that book to me not to you!'

Legal rights obviously presuppose the existence of a legal system of some kind though presumably many of them originated in tradition. It is equally obvious that legal rights vary between places and times. In modern Western nations these rights cannot be added or subtracted merely at the whim of a King or a President.

Rights based on law are usually restricted to certain classes of people, they depend on status or age or qualifications. In Western nations the right to marry depends on having reached a certain age and on not being married already. The right to an old age pension exists only in wealthier nations and depends on reaching 55 or 60 or 65 (whatever). In some Middle Eastern countries the right to drive a car depends on being male, while in other parts of the world that right depends on being adult, or nearly adult, and on having passed a driving test.

Civil rights can be thought of as a special type of legal right. It is possible to draw two formal distinctions between civil rights and the other legal rights. First, civil rights are held by all (adult) citizens whereas other legal rights depend on age, status and so on. Secondly, civil rights have to do with the defence of other rights. They are in some sense *rights about rights*. Choosing a government in a democracy helps ensure that ordinary legal rights are respected; the right to vote, therefore, relates to the protection of other rights. The right to test a claim to a special right (for example a property right) in a court of law is another right relating to rights.

Although civil rights are often referred to in constitutional documents they also exist in countries which have no written constitutions. Thus 'the British Constitution' is not the name of a document but refers to a collection of laws and customarily binding precedents which (mainly) have to do with supra-legal and political rights. These laws and precedents, which happened to enter the political system at different times in the history of the nation, resemble the provisions of modern Bills of Rights. They can be found in Magna Carta, in the Act of Parliament of 1807 which abolished the slave trade in British colonies and on British ships, in the Reform Bills of 1832, 1867 and 1884, and in the legislation of 1919 and 1928 which gave votes to women.

Natural rights are generally described as absolute and universal. They are held to belong to all members of the human race without exception. The English philosophers Thomas Hobbes (1588–1679) and John Locke (1632–1704) both argue that men have natural rights because of their natural equality as members of the same species.

More importantly the theory of natural rights involves a view about *the purpose of the State* – which in turn gives a way of distinguishing legitimate from illegitimate forms of government.

It is agreed by philosophers who believe in natural rights that these include the right to life and the right to liberty. John Locke added property to the list, Thomas Jefferson added the pursuit of happiness, and the French Constitution mentions security and the right to resist oppression.

'Nonsense on Stilts'?

In the twentieth century the notion of natural rights has been attacked by moral philosophers as 'too abstract'. Natural rights, it is said, cannot exist because they are intangible, unscientific and ineffective.

However, natural rights are not more abstract than the other concepts investigated by moral philosophers. Duty, virtue and value itself, are all abstract concepts. Abstract notions do indeed refer to intangibles but the idea that only the tangible is 'real' is crude and false. Numbers are intangible yet without numbers there would be no physical science and the kind of life lived by physicists, their way of existing, would disappear. For ways of thinking are also ways of existing. If the concept of natural rights

24

were to vanish a certain way of thinking about people and government would vanish with it – and also a certain way of existing.

Discourse about natural rights is only nonsense if conceived (wrongly) as analogous to discourse about the natural body, with its natural functions, natural life span, natural sleep patterns and so on. But rights, obviously, are not bodies or organs or organic functions. In a moral or political context the word natural means: *pertaining to creatures in virtue of their species or type and not because of artificial or social characteristics.* Here the word *natural* is simply the opposite of special, social, restricted, legal. This explains why natural rights and universal human rights are interchangeable expressions.

In calling some rights natural one implies that they are logically prior to the rights created by laws and different from the rights held only by certain specified social groups.

The idea of natural rights appears or reappears at times when people come to believe that the laws made by their governments are unjust or rest on corrupt practices, or, in general, make life worse rather than better for the citizens. The reason for having governments in the first place, and for putting up with state officials and laws and taxes, is not to make one's life worse! If legal rights do not cater for human needs, if they are allocated only to people of status or wealth (as has in fact been the case for most of human history), those without status or wealth have no reason, other than tradition and fear, to respect them. Rights which are neither universal, nor aimed at fulfilling some important or useful social purpose, merely reflect the power of the powerful. This is why philosophers such as Locke and Hobbes hold that the validity of ordinary law rests in the end on the premise that there are fundamental universal rights. The notion that some things are owed to all human beings purely in virtue of being human is the bedrock premise needed to guarantee the legitimacy and reasonableness of laws and governments.

History shows that the idea of natural rights has been very influential. Of course there are countries in which natural rights and civil rights and even ordinary legal rights are ignored, but that does not prove that the idea is ineffective everywhere. Dictatorships are unlikely to respect rights or even their own constitutions, yet tyrants sometimes accept, or even set up, national constitutions which appear to guarantee human rights. This is hypocrisy, the tribute which vice pays to virtue.

PART TWO

A Defence of Humanism

CHAPTER FOUR

Human Beings and Persons

'. . . he has been abolished; he has become an unperson'

George Orwell, *1984*

Utilitarians and Personists

The idea that all human beings share certain fundamental rights is nowadays often attacked by philosophy teachers. It might seem strange that it is the self-styled liberals, and not the self-styled conservatives, who are hostile to the idea of universal human rights. Strange, because the concept of universal human rights is essentially egalitarian in character, and it is liberals, rather than conservatives, who uphold egalitarian doctrines. Conservatives do not disapprove of hierarchies. The situation looks less strange, however, when one remembers that liberals often take a utilitarian position in ethics. Their antagonism towards the notion of universal human rights is inherited from Jeremy Bentham, he who (as we saw) described the concept of natural rights as 'nonsense on stilts'.

Philosophy teachers hostile to the idea of universal rights draw a distinction between two different kinds of human being, as follows. Human *persons* are those who currently possess certain mental capacities, whereas other human beings, for example infants who have not yet developed these mental capacities, or the old and the ill who have lost them, are not persons. According to this premise persons must be accorded respect and dignity, and even rights, but other human beings need not be so regarded.

I label those who believe in this doctrine *personists* because the distinction they draw is always flagged by the word *person*. Thus in his book *Practical Ethics* (p. 124) Peter Singer says:

> Bentham was right to describe infanticide as 'of a nature not to cause the slightest inquietude to the most timid imagination' [because] we can see that the grounds for not killing persons do not apply to newborn infants . . . a newborn baby is not an autonomous being . . . and so to kill it cannot violate the principle of respect for autonomy.

Singer adds:

> The fact that a being is a human being, in the sense of a member of the species *homo sapiens*, is not relevant to the wrongness of killing it . . .

Philosophy teachers deeply influenced by what I have called personism include Michael Tooley, Ronald Dworkin and Jonathan Glover. Those who are opposed to personism, who hold that being human is a morally significant fact, I shall call *humanists*.

Note that personism must be distinguished both from personalism and *personalismo*.

Personalism is a type of religious humanism which can be traced to writings by Bohne, Muenier and Berdyaev. It entails belief in a personal god and respect for human life; respect is owed to man because it is owed to God. The word personalism is often used by Pope John Paul II.

The concept of *personalismo* comes to us from South America and means a type of political loyalty which attaches not to policies but to leaders.

Personism is, in a sense, the opposite of personalism. *Personal-*

ism insists that all human life must be respected whereas *personism* claims that human life as such is not worthy of respect; only *some* human beings have rights and are worthy of respect. In other words, personist philosophy says that the wrongness of killing beings has nothing to do with their being human. It states that individual human beings have a right to life if and only if they are persons in a certain philosophical sense, if and only if they come up to some specified standard of knowledge, skill or mental qualities. Lost skills and merely potential behaviour are alike regarded as irrelevant and potentialities in particular are seen as being of little account; hence personists believe that young infants are not persons and can be destroyed if no one wants them.

The general standard for personhood usually adopted by currently fashionable philosophy teachers is as follows: a person is a thinking, intelligent being in possession of reason, reflection, memory and awareness of self. Some add the condition that in order to be a person one must also understand the (i.e., their) concept of a person.

Quite a few human beings fail to live up to the stringent conditions demanded by personism. Some people are too young to have memories, some suffer amnesia, some are senile, some are in a coma, some are not sane, many are unreflective, and reason and intelligence vary greatly from one individual to another.

The concept of supernatural beings whose essence lies in their spiritual and mental capacities is quite ancient. This historic notion lies buried deep inside the current distinction drawn between human beings and persons.

Philosophy teachers in the twentieth century defend the supposed validity of the person *versus* human distinction mainly by quoting one another – for example, Peter Singer quotes Jonathan Glover and both Singer and Ronald Dworkin quote Michael Tooley – but they also refer back to the authority of John Locke, whose disquisition on personal identity begins with a short account of the identity of God.

31

Humanism and Religion

Personists in general argue that special respect for human life is not rational because it rests on unproven religious dogmas. They infer that it must be illogical for non-religious people to be humanists; non-religious people, they say, ought to be personists, like them. They condemn the protection of infant life and the lives of the elderly because they believe the desire for such protection is a distinctively Christian attitude. Peter Singer, for example, claims that the intrinsic value of human life is an idea which began with

> Christian insistence on the importance of species membership: the belief that all born of human parents are immortal and destined for an eternity of bliss or for everlasting torment.

This remark betrays a certain ignorance of Judaism, and of ancient Greek philosophers such as the Pythagoreans. It also sidesteps the biological facts that help to make sense of the idea that our human lives are intrinsically valuable.

To take the first point first: the Mosaic commandment 'thou shalt not kill' predates Christianity by many centuries. (According to the editors of the Jerusalem Bible Moses lived 1,200 years before Christ; and King Josiah, whose priests rediscovered the Book of the Law, lived 660 years before Christ.) Respect for human life is one of the foundations of traditional Jewish law, it is a bedrock belief expressed not only in the commandment but also in the Hebrews' condemnation of human sacrifice to be seen in (for example) Leviticus 18: 21 and 2. Kings 23: 10 (King James Bible). This bedrock belief also manifests itself in the severe punishments decreed for those who harm pregnant women, mentioned in Exodus 21: 22–4. Moreover Jewish respect for human life cannot be based on an anticipation of immortality because immortality is not an absolutely central tenet of Judaism.

32

Not all Jewish sects have believed in eternal life. It is well known that the Sadducees rejected that idea.

The followers of Pythagoras forbade the taking of life; they were opposed both to suicide and to abortion.

Philosophical theses are not like the prepacked assortments of salad vegetables to be found in supermarkets. Philosophy does not come prepackaged and no reasoning which assumes a 'supermarket salad' view can be intellectually respectable. It is always possible to consider philosophical theses one by one. Propositions which do not contradict one another can be combined in different ways. From the point of view of logic the proposition that human life has intrinsic value is not inextricably connected to a particular religion, nor indeed to any religion. It is consistent both with religious humanism and with agnostic and atheistic humanism.

The horror felt at the spectacle of atrocities such as 'ethnic cleansing' is a human horror, not a religious one.

As to the second point: biologists know that all animals behave in ways that tend to preserve their own species and that gregarious creatures bond naturally with members of their own type. Anthropologists know that human beings everywhere nurture their young and look after the old. War and poverty can affect these instinctive practices but that does not mean that they are not beneficial. It is true that some human groups, such as the Inuit in the past, and the Trobriand Islanders of the nineteenth century (beset as these were by an influx of ruthless, wealthy Western whites), lived in situations of stress and poverty and other difficulties and for those reasons decided to invent ways of shortening some lives. But these facts about communities in stress cannot possibly provide a reason for shortening lives elsewhere.

Personists are often utilitarians, hence their bedrock beliefs have to do with the pleasant and painful consequences of social policies and individual actions. As we have already seen this bedrock is unsatisfactory because the estimation of short-term consequences is difficult and estimation of long-term results is impossible. Utilitarianism rests on guesswork.

The Philosophy of Locke

Let us now consider John Locke's conception of personhood.

Locke defines a person as a being with reason, consciousness (including self-consciousness) and memories. In his view the identity of a person over time depends partly on reason and consciousness and partly on having, or rather on being, a set of relatively coherent, relatively connected (overlapping) memories. It follows from Locke's account that one person, or set of memories, could have two living bodies, and that one living body could at different times contain two different persons. It also follows that creatures other than human beings, parrots for instance, or aliens from outer space, could turn out to be persons.

Locke argues, rather confusedly, that a man is not the same kind of entity as a person. At some points he appears to say that persons and men belong in different categories: one is a living substance, the other is a set of mental events and capacities. Yet since a man can have or possess such capacities he can also, according to Locke, be a person as well as being a man.

Perhaps Locke's concept is best thought of as analogous to the concept of a role. A role is not an entity but different entities can take on the same roles and conversely the same entity might take on different roles.

Locke says that men, like trees, are living beings whose individual identities are constituted by material bodies which persist through time and 'share in the same life' over time. A man is a living animal with a continuing uninterrupted existence governed by the laws of growth and decay for animal (human) bodies.

Now: if a living creature possesses mental capacities of the right kind it will be a person as well as an animal. Human beings considered as a species are of course capable of reason, and capable of remembering things, but those facts about the capacities of the race do not suffice to guarantee that a particular individual is a person in (what seems to be) Locke's sense. Particular individuals can lose the power to reason, as sometimes happens during senescence, or might not have any memoris at all, as must be the case with newborn infants. In such cases, it seems, Locke would say that personhood is absent.

The ethical consequences, however, are not serious for him, nor are his moral conclusions counter-intuitive for us; for the following reasons:

Having drawn a distinction between persons, on the one hand, and mankind on the other, Locke remains completely unequivocal about which side of the division contains the bearers of rights. It is the natural equality of human beings, not any supposed or actual equality of persons, which constitutes the foundation of his theory of natural law.

In *An Essay Concerning the True Original Extent and End of Civil Government* he says:

> There [is] nothing more evident than that creatures of the same species should also be equal amongst one another . . . [and] the equality of men by Nature . . . is . . . beyond all question.

Locke explains natural rights as follows:

> The state of nature has a law of nature to govern it, and reason, which is that law, teaches all mankind, who will but consult it, that being all equal and independent, no one ought to harm another in his life, liberty, health or possessions.

Modern personist philosophers, on the other hand, jump the other way. Their theoretical distinction between human beings and persons resembles Locke's to some extent, but, unlike his, its purpose is to draw a line between those innocent human beings who must not be killed and those who (allegedly) need not be treated with respect because they do not have a right to life.

Definitions of 'person'

According to the *Oxford English Dictionary* the meaning of the word *person* comes from the Latin *persona*, meaning a mask or a character in a play.

In England 500 years ago the word had come to signify either an agent, that is, an individual acting in some capacity or other, or a human being as opposed to any other kind of animal. The second of these senses is now predominant in ordinary speech.

In law a distinction is drawn between natural persons (human beings) and artificial persons (corporations, trade unions, colleges and the like).

There is also of course the grammatical sense in which *we*, *you*, *they*, are instances of the first, second and third person respectively.

Some dictionaries list a 'philosophical' sense of the word, defining it in the way Locke does.

Finally, the word exists as a technical term in zoology. In zoology persons are 'individuals in a colonial organism such as coral'.

Clearly the word *person* is by no means univocal. Nevertheless it is fairly obvious that in ordinary everyday life persons and human beings are taken to be the same things. Philosophy students, for instance, always use the terms *human being* and *person* interchangeably until they are taught not to by their philosophy teachers. Even after hearing many lectures on the subject some students continue, absent-mindedly perhaps, to misread and misquote Locke's account of personhood, possibly because deep down they just can't believe that anyone would really want to draw a line between personhood and humanity. Dictionaries support the students' intuitions rather than the professors' teachings, for, as we have seen, the predominant sense of this contested word just is: *human beings in general.*

In most kinds of enquiry there can arise a need for semi-technical terms, or for new definitions, as elements ordained to fill a role in a system. In philosophy the word *person* has been just such a term. The original need for this special term was theological, having to do with the Christian concept of the Holy Trinity. Its migration into ethics is a relatively recent phenomenon. Deciding to concentrate wholly on the most prescriptive of the several senses of *person* would not be unreasonable for those working in the history of seventeenth-century philosophy; not really unreasonable for those puzzled by the mystery of consciousness, since the semi-technical or Lockean sense depends on the notion of memory; not entirely unreasonable for those interested in the problems of identity; but arbitrary, and dangerous, in ethical and political philosophy. To pre-empt the great questions of human worth and natural rights on the basis of a specialized definition which ignores ordinary usage cannot but be arbitrary! That these questions have indeed been pre-empted in an arbitrary way is demonstrated, in my opinion, by the immediate and most important outcome of contemporary theories resting on the so-called philosophical definition of a person: namely, the flat denial of universal human rights.

It is the ordinary (or most common) sense of the word which has moral import because morality, if it exists for the sake of anything, exists for the sake of human beings, not for the benefit of a class of rational entities picked out by a philosopher's definition. Moreover Locke himself, as we have already noticed, held that morality has to do with *human* welfare.

Personism and Justice

Concentration on the special 'philosophical' sense of the word person too often generates egregious errors of fact. Thus in the great *Encyclopedia of Philosophy* (ed. Paul Edwards) the entry on persons (written by Arthur Danto, a well-known philosophy professor) contains an egregious error of fact about the law:

A Defence of Humanism

a person simply is any being having legal rights and duties. But in this respect not every human being is legally a person (children and idiots are not persons) . . .

In British, American and European legal systems, however, children and idiots *are* persons. Unlike animals, children and idiots cannot be locked up without due process; they can own property; to kill them is murder; and their property rights and the right not to be killed or locked up, can all be defended in the courts. Having juridical rights is the same thing as being a legal person.

Since the word *person* is not univocal it can be asked: Why do contemporary moral philosophers choose to discuss only one of its several senses? Is it possible for philosophers to discover what persons really are, to discover the true nature of persons, if they confine their attention to a single, specialized, and in part merely prescriptive, definition? Is their choice reasonable, or arbitrary and unreasonable?

As noted earlier, the most significant outcome of theories which rest on the prescriptive or philosophical definition is a flat denial that human life has any special moral significance and a flat denial of universal human rights. Now, the concept of universal human rights is based on the idea of equality. Nevertheless some of those who believe themselves to be upholders of natural rights, who would not dream of attacking that notion, adhere implicitly, perhaps even unconsciously, to the quite different attitude that, while they and their friends have rights, inferior types, such as women, or children, or blacks, or the mentally ill, do not. The American *Declaration of Independence* is a stirring defence of natural rights, yet several of its signatories were slave owners. Moreover they and their successors refused, for 150 years, to give women the same legal rights as men. The American philosophy professor Ronald Dworkin expresses much patriotic devotion to the Constitution of the USA and to the *Declaration of Independence* while at the same time arguing that very young children, and seriously disabled adults, do not have quite the same sort of right to life as he does himself.

Justice has to be founded on the axiom that everyone has the same basic or natural rights. Otherwise justice, so-called, will favour rich men and other strong people, and at worst will uphold the interests of the few who rule against the many who are ruled.

Moreover 'everyone' has to mean every human being, not every 'person' as defined by philosophers. The distinction between human beings and other things is natural, not arbitrary, and not difficult to draw either in principle or in practice. But the differences between levels of intelligence, between having coherent or incoherent memories, between being sane and insane, and so on, are matters of degree, not of kind. Worse still, these differences often have a social dimension, they are defined in ways that reflect cultural as well as biological facts. Perceived differences in intellectual ability, for example, vary from place to place and from time to time and depend to a considerable extent on what fashionable psychology, or society at large, regards as a reliable test or indicator. Finally the differences, even when considered naturalistically, are not commensurable with one another. Is an individual of high intelligence suffering from amnesia more or less of a person than someone with low intelligence and a good memory? Does a man in a temporary coma turn into a person only when he wakes up? How wakeful must he be? Any distinction between Lockean persons and Lockean non-persons will be extremely difficult to draw, both in practice and in theory, because each of the differences upon which the distinction relies is a difference of quantity lying on a sliding scale and the scales are not commensurate. To determine in a particular case whether or not some individual is a 'person in a philosophical sense' necessarily requires the making of *ad hoc* decisions about boundaries. Now in some areas of life arbitrary decisions are perfectly legitimate. There is nothing wrong with drawing an arbitrary line between bald men and not-bald men, for example

– which is just as well since there is no other way to draw it. The decision to give the title of Grand Master to chess players who have achieved this or that norm is also essentially arbitrary; the norm could be made higher, or lower, and provided chess players in general agreed no harm would be done. But justice is different. A system in which legal decisions were arbitrary would not be justice at all. Justice itself cannot be made the subject of an arbitrary definition. We cannot simply decree that from now on justice is going to consist of rules made in the interest of politicians and their friends, or for the benefit of whites, or for the sake of making life easy for healthy adults, or because of a simplifying and simplistic desire to downgrade human infants too young to speak by grouping them with apes and dolphins, creatures which also cannot speak. On the contrary all our intuitions tell us that justice, to be that, must work for weak human beings as well as for strong ones.

There are fundamental differences between an ethics which acknowledges that human lives as such have value, which treats this proposition as bedrock, and an ethics which claims that value, and rights, belong only to those beings who are currently capable of these or those exercises of intellect, or memory, or other arbitrarily chosen mental activities. A peculiar view about what counts as justice is one of the distinguishing marks of personism.

CHAPTER FIVE

Human Beings and the Other Animals

'The just man is compassionate to his beasts; but the heart of the wicked is cruel.'

Proverbs

Beliefs about the ethical treatment of animals tend to take two extreme forms. According to one set of extremists human beings have no moral obligations whatsoever towards members of other species. Philosophers who have defended this view include René Descartes, who believed (wrongly of course) that animals are non-sentient machines, and Baruch Spinoza. The anti-animal extremism of Spinoza and Descartes was rejected by other thinkers, notably Leibniz, Voltaire and Kant. In the nineteenth and twentieth centuries many biologists have held extreme anti-animal opinions, presumably because their research projects and research moneys involved experimentation on animals. It should be noted, though, that during the late twentieth century British university students studying biology and related sciences have objected (and with some success) to excessive, or even any, use of laboratory animals in teaching programmes. The other extreme can be seen in the dictum, expressed by Peter Singer: 'All Animals are Equal . . . Supporters of Liberation for Blacks and Women Should Support Animal Liberation as Well.' Singer seriously believes his slogan, arguing that 'speciesism', like racism and sexism, is a bad thing. As a personist he rejects the idea that human life (or any life) has intrinsic value: as an animal

41

liberationist he holds that human lives are not necessarily of more value than the lives of, say, dolphins and chimpanzees. His belief that human life is not necessarily more valuable than the lives of other creatures is one of the reasons why he supports the legalization of infanticide and euthanasia.

Most people will probably feel that neither extreme is correct. No one, apart from a few entrepreneurs and scientists, really believes that it is all right for experimental biologists to cause as much suffering to sentient non-human creatures as they feel like or judge fitting. On the other hand no one, apart from a few philosophy teachers, seriously believes that allowing a jungle tiger to starve is just as bad as allowing the tiger to stalk and eat a human baby.

'Speciesism'

Students influenced by personist philosophy teachers do not always question the proposition that 'speciesism' is a bad kind of 'ism' like sexism or racism or chauvinism. They don't consider the possibility that it is a good 'ism' like (perhaps) egalitarianism and patriotism.

Speciesism is merely a word. Inventing and using a new word cannot by itself show that it is wrong for human beings to think of human beings as special. Not all 'isms' are bad: if they were then 'lifeism' would be bad. ('Lifeism', of course, is the idea that animate creatures are more important, from the moral point of view, than sticks and stones.) We should remember that speciesism is a term of art which has been repeatedly used for the purpose of downgrading the importance of human life. We should remember that a mere word cannot be made to bear the enormous weight of the radical conclusion that being human has no special significance.

Sociologists and anthropologists have coined the word *pseudo-speciation* to describe the attitudes of those who believe, or seem to believe, that people of different races and different colours actually belong to different species. The attitudes of those who accept pseudo-speciation are, of course, mistaken, since human beings are genetically similar to one another and genetically distinct from our nearest evolutionary relatives, the great apes. We could coin another word, *pseudo-raciation* perhaps, to describe the mistaken belief that species differences are of no greater importance than the differences between races.

There is some analogy between 'speciesism' and racism, perhaps: but how much?

Respect for the Living and the Dead

Let us compare meat-eating with cannibalism. Most people find the idea of cannibalism abhorrent – and most people (in the West) eat meat. Is the difference between the two kinds of food merely imaginary? If 'speciesism' really *is* wrong there would be nothing wrong with cannibalism in itself. Domestic animals are killed deliberately, not accidentally, and often in conditions of some cruelty, but healthy human beings, on the other hand, are very often killed in accidents. If 'speciesism' really *is* a bad thing it must be wrong to eat animals which have been deliberately (and painfully) killed but perfectly all right to eat the human (and animal) victims of traffic accidents. Most people find the idea of eating members of their own species quite appalling – but any consistent anti-'speciesist' should refuse to eat commercial beef and mutton and chicken while not blanching at the thought of eating people killed in traffic accidents.

Anti-'speciesist' philosophy teachers claim that special reverence and respect for human beings and for the human body is merely irrational. Hence, from the point of view of these theorists abhorrence at the idea of eating human flesh must also be irrational.

The reason civilized people do not eat human accident victims is that they are not cannibals and part of not being a cannibal consists in respect for the human dead. Respect for the human dead is an anti-cannibalistic attitude. This respect is doubtless an aspect of the innate preference which human beings, like other gregarious creatures, feel for members of their own species.

When great respect as well as compassion is shown to members of other species the reason is usually religious. Thus stray dogs are welcomed into the Buddhist monasteries of India, Bhutan and Tibet because they are believed to be reincarnations of worldly or doggish monks returning to their old abodes. In ancient Egypt cats were objects of worship and for that reason their dead bodies were mummified and preserved like the bodies of the Pharoahs. It is when animals are thought to share either a human or a divine nature that their dead bodies are treated with special respect. In my opinion 'funeral ceremonies' carried out for pet animals in the West are rather like solemn games; they are intended to console children and childlike adults.

(I should mention, though, that Cora Diamond disagrees with this view. She objects that animals and human beings can be friends and one does not make a solemn game out of a friend's funeral. Professor Diamond goes on to quote Edmund Blunden's translation of a rather touching ancient Greek verse about a dead dog:

> He came from Malta, and Eumelis says
> He had no dog like him in all his days;
> We called him Bull; he went into the dark;
> Along those roads we cannot hear him bark.

Innate Preferences

It is natural for gregarious creatures to prefer the members of their own species and human beings are no exception to the rule. Human beings bond with one another naturally and this is doubtless the biological and psychological basis of morality – a fact which moral philosophers ought not to forget. It is true, of course, that inter-species bonding is also possible. It occurs very noticeably in the relationships between dogs and people, horses and people, and even cats and people. We could perhaps think of inter-species bonding as the biological basis which makes it possible for thoughtful individuals to take a moral view of their pets and other animals.

Yet even very sensitive pro-animal people find it difficult to think of humanity as an 'ordinary' species.

Although sensitive Westerners, for example, do not eat their pets they do kill them, sometimes, when they are ill, and they also kill unwanted puppies and kittens (painlessly of course). These killings are not hedged around with discretionary or other restrictions. On the other hand even personist philosophy teachers, even members of the euthanasia lobby, always hedge (human) euthanasia with discretionary (or other) restrictions. Do they insist on those restrictions merely for PR reasons? I wonder . . .

Secondly, there is a difference between the way sensitive Westerners think about endangered species and the way they think about the human species. Nowadays rare animals are not hunted in Britain (or not legally) because many influential people have decreed that endangered species – not endangered individuals – must be protected. Preservation of rare animals is quite different from preservation of human beings. It is not motivated by thoughts about the rights of individual eagles and tigers and elephants. The project of protection, in other words, is not based on the notion that individual animals have rights just like human rights. (Nor is the desire to preserve endangered species always motivated by self-seeking human needs.) Moreover such preservation is consistent with the idea, which does not strike most animal lovers as obnoxious, that some of the more common species (rats, mosquitoes) are vermin whose numbers must be kept in check. The idea that some kinds of people are vermin, on the other hand, is not accepted by (most) animal lovers.

Thirdly, we human beings differentiate not only between ourselves and 'the rest', but also among 'the rest'. This differentiation isn't made merely on the basis of what we know about the intelligence and sentience of various creatures. It is to some extent a cultural matter. Horses, dogs, cats and cage birds have a special place in human life, a place which we gave them. We treat dogs differently from monkeys (which are more intelligent) and also differently from sheep (which are less). In Hindu countries the cow is sacred and must not be killed and the ox is sacred because it is the son of the cow. British people eat cows but they don't eat horses. Our reasons are not philosophical but have to do with the fact that we have made friends with horses and not with cows. We eat pigs, which are more intelligent than horses or cows or cats.

Anti-'speciesists' are silent on these various cultural practices which, to be consistent, they ought to condemn.

Is There Anything Special About Us?

Is there anything special about the human species? Well, in the first place it is *our* species. All the gregarious animals on Earth instinctively prefer their own species, stay together in groups, and care for and protect their young. Species-preference is both natural and valuable. It is needed for survival. From our human point of view there is nothing wrong whatsoever with preferring the human species. If the preference disappeared completely then most likely humanity itself would disappear too.

There are good consequentialist reasons why people ought to support some degree of 'speciesism'. If people try to treat animals and human beings alike the main result, in the real world, will be, not that animals will be treated with more respect than they are at present, but that human beings will be treated with less. Perhaps that doesn't have to be so but experience of the real world shows that it just *is* so. The case of personist philosophy itself also shows it is so. Not all personists are vegetarians; which shows that the influence, in the real world, of this type of philosophy is less likely to engender respect for animals than to withdraw respect from human beings.

Human beings are different from the other animals. Perhaps the most striking difference is that the other animals adapt, in Darwinian fashion, to the environments in which they find themselves, whereas the human animal continually creates new environments for itself (and for the other species). These created environments are extremely various. There is the igloo environment and the mud hut environment and the aeroplane and the supermarket and the farm and the factory and the cathedral and the hospital and the university. Human beings also create environments in which they themselves cannot survive: the minefield and the nuclear testing ground, for example. Human beings create different kinds of social and moral environments too. Some social and moral environments are hostile to individuals or to groups or races or minorities. A moral and social environment based on an extreme anti-'speciesism' is pretty likely to be hostile to quite a few human beings.

Is there a purely objective 'gods'-eye' point of view which lies beyond and above our human perspective? Can philosophers produce such a view? That seems very doubtful. Theorizing is a human activity. Moral philosophy is a human activity. Consequentialism, for example, is a theory in which certain human beings attribute value to the results of actions, and (traditionally) to nothing else. Nowadays, as we have seen, it is often combined with personism, a theory in which certain human beings attribute value to intellect, memory and consciousness and not much else. Such theories might ignore or downgrade our species but in so far as they are themselves the products of human thinking they cannot claim to give a gods'-eye view.

A moral agent is a human being and as such lives in a world of value. Value is not itself a simple biological fact and our moral attitudes to animals do not rest solely or even largely on per-ceived biological similarities and differences. They are deter-

47

mined partly by culture, 'by what we have made of the difference between us and animals' (Cora Diamond). As we have seen, dogs and cats are special in the West while cows and their sons are special in India. Several races and nations see the horse as a beautiful spirited animal which must not be hunted or eaten. Animals have been treated as companions, as religious objects, as symbols, and as workers. Some see them as analogous to valuable art (the snow leopard) or again as beautiful things to possess (peacocks, goldfish). As far as I know all nations have myths and stories about animals.

Sentience and intelligence enter into the world of value as only two elements among many. The moral principles we adopt in regard to animals don't stand stark naked (as in extremist pro-animal or anti-animal philosophies) but are clothed, as it were, with culture. It is partly because they ignore the fact that human beings create cultures and live in a world of value that 'stark naked' pro-animal principles lead, in the real world, to disrespect for humans rather than to respect for animals.

Cruelty and Compassion

The only important similarity between racism and sexism, on the one hand, and 'speciesism', on the other, consists in a blindness to cruelty. To hold that cruelty can only be condemned on account of the supposed reason that 'speciesism' is bad, is to put the cart before the horse. We don't need a reason for thinking cruelty is bad but we do need a reason for thinking 'speciesism' is bad.

In America before the abolition of slavery black people were forced to endure great physical and mental cruelty. It was illegal in the southern states to teach a slave to read and write. Slaves were treated like farm animals, branded like horses and cows, and used for breeding more slaves. Charles Dickens notes (in *Martin*

Chuzzlewit) that some white men were happy to sell their own half-caste offspring in slave markets. Women everywhere have had to endure quite a lot of mental cruelty; a subtle description of such is to be found in George Eliot's novel *The Mill on the Floss*, in which the heroine, Maggie Tulliver, who longs to learn, and is far more intelligent than her brother Tom, is not allowed to study.

Parallels with the way animals are treated are fairly clear. Hunting is a cruel and unnecessary practice. Factory farming is cruel. Slaughter of animals for food is in many countries carried out in cruel ways. That wild animals in cages suffer something closely akin to mental cruelty has long been obvious to all but the most insensitive human observers.

Conclusions

Precise conclusions about how to act are hard to come by in this area, at least in the present state of philosophy. It seems fairly clear that both kinds of extremism – the pro-animal as well as the anti-animal – are wrong. On the one hand we know for a fact that animals are not insentient machines, we know that cruelty is bad, we know that cruelty is only possible in actions directed at sentient beings. On the other hand if we hold that human life is a bedrock value we will agree that it is partly because animals resemble *us* that we owe them moral concern.

The higher animals resemble us not only in being sentient but in several other ways as well. We recognize many non-physical properties in dogs and horses and perhaps in other creatures too – loyalty, for example, and companionability and helpfulness. There are many examples of pets who save their masters from wicked people or natural disasters and who mourn on the graves of human friends. In fairy-tales human speech is attributed to the other creatures, men turn into frogs and vice versa, and Beauty eventually marries the Beast who is a Prince under a spell. Hindus and Buddhists believe that human lives and animal lives are linked in reincarnation.

Given that both forms of extremism are wrong we can say that there must be 'a queue of moral concern' (Mary Midgley). Our problem is to arrange the queue. This is not an easy task. Placing human beings at the head of the queue is only the beginning: how are we to rank the apes and the dolphins and the whales and the tigers and our domestic pets? How much weight should we give to cultural factors? Won't our own human lives be seriously impoverished if we ignore cultural factors? Finally, it is agreed on all sides that our moral obligations belong to us because we are human. Is that itself a 'speciesist' theory?

I shall have to leave these questions about the queue for readers to think about and answer if they can. But here is a final question. Is it because humanity is no more important than the other animals that we should be compassionate to them? Or is it because we are higher than they are?

CHAPTER SIX

Human Beings and Machines

'Although we are mere sojourners on the surface of the planet, chained to a mere point in space, enduring but for a moment of time, the human mind is enabled not only to number worlds beyond the unassisted ken of mortal eye, but to trace the events of indefinite ages before the creation of our race, and is not even withheld from penetrating into the dark secrets of the ocean or the interior of the solid globe . . .'

Charles Lyell, *Principles of Geology*

Reductive Philosophy and Occam's Razor

William of Occam (1300–48) proposed that the following rule be adopted when theorizing: *Do not multiply entities beyond necessity.* For example, if some phenomenon can be explained by postulating one cause there is no need to postulate two or three or more causes; the superfluous postulations should be razored away.

Reductive philosophy employs a generalized version of the Razor. A reductive ontology asks: What is everything made out of? Ancient answers include *All is water*, and *All is fire*. A more up-to-date reply would be *Everything is made of electrons*. In the philosophy of language a reductive strategist might try to show that the basic 'atoms' of meaning are sentences, or words, or names, or labels, or marks on paper, or noises made by mouths.

Philosophical reductionism, or nothing-but-ism, appeals very strongly to a certain kind of temperament. Thinkers who wish to say 'the world is nothing but such-and-such' often like to add 'and language is nothing but . . .', 'morality is nothing but . . .', 'so-called truth is nothing but . . .', and so on.

A reductive philosophy which is concerned with living creatures is likely to have ethical implications. Consequentialism, for example, reduces ethical thinking to the calculation of possible results and when it is combined with personism it generates the conclusion that there is nothing specially valuable about human beings.

Reductive theories, whether ontological, epistemological or ethical, often turn out to be inadequate. The unwise use of Occam's Razor cuts off too much.

This chapter will discuss a currently popular view of the nature of human thought processes, namely, the theory that human thinking is nothing but a more complicated version of what goes on inside a computer.

The idea that human beings, or human brains, resemble sophisticated bits of machinery has been greatly bolstered by the armchair speculations of philosophers involved with cognitive science. The implications, for ethical theory, of these speculations seem to hold no interest for cognitive scientists. Yet it is fair to say, I believe, that the ontology of the machine tends to encourage the view that the sanctity of human life is a mere superstition. For very often the overall psychological effect of breaking down a distinction is to reduce respect for one side of the distinction. If one knows that living matter is made up of carbon and oxygen and hydrogen one might find oneself asking: Is there anything ethically important about carbon? Or oxygen? What's so important, then, about living things? In short, a philosophy which speculates that human thought and thinking are reducible to the same kind of operations that occur in computers is not *logically* inconsistent with respect for human life but its *psychological* effect tends in that direction. That is because in such a philosophy the concept of human thinking is analysed in ways that do not mention life. However, there are good reasons for believing that a correct analysis of human thinking has to mention human life.

52

Machines and Metaphors

One important style of reductive philosophy about the nature of thought begins with Alan Turing's famous paper, published in the journal *Mind* in 1950, in which he states that the essence of thinking is the ability to give correct answers to certain sorts of question. Turing believed, apparently, that thinking either is, or is whatever produces, the ability to answer questions in mathematics and logic. In his paper he reasons as follows. Imagine that a human being and a Universal Computing Machine are placed in a closed room (the 'Turing Room'), with apparatus for sending and receiving written messages to and from an observer outside. The observer sends in questions and the man and the machine send back separate written replies. Turing says that the observer outside would not be able to tell which replies came from the machine and which from the man. He concludes that both the man and the machine would be thinking.

What is wrong with this picture? Well, we might object that to talk of machines thinking is to speak in metaphor and we might compare this metaphor with others. For example: men run on two legs, dogs run on four legs, and fish, who have no legs, cannot run at all; but water, which has no legs, and is not even alive, can run downhill. Some other legless and inanimate things – engines – can run without changing location!

The running of water and of engines is obviously metaphorical because real running, the paradigm of running, is running with legs. By parallel reasoning, it seems, we can argue that any account of non-metaphorical thinking must start with the paradigm case. Now the paradigm case here is human thinking and human thinking is part of human life. D. H. Mellor notes that the question whether computers can think is interesting only if it is directed at finding out which operations of computers resemble the operations of a human mind.

No doubt some readers will agree that the thinking of computers is like running without legs while others will insist that computers think in the literal sense. The reasons offered for the second, or Turingesque, opinion are fairly familiar. Modern computers perform tasks with great rapidity and so reach solutions not available to a human being in a human lifetime. Given a little help from hackers and other human operators modern computers can 'communicate' with one another. Modern computers have feedback. Neurologists and biochemists tell us that brains, like computers, process information. We are told, too, that brains and computers seem to work in somewhat similar ways.

Those who hold that machine thinking is a metaphor will perhaps respond by saying that genuine thinking requires consciousness.

Consciousness and Information-processing

Common sense tells us that consciousness is present in many living creatures: horses and dogs, seagulls and mice, and perhaps even ants and bees, are conscious. Do these animals think? Consciousness might be a precondition of thought but it isn't exactly the same thing. If a creature is thinking many would say that it must be conscious, but few, I believe, would make the opposite inference.

Entities which process information comprise a considerable variety. Some processors of information are thinkers who think while processing, others can think but do not necessarily think while processing, and others never think at all. Processors include complete animals and also parts of animals. Human beings and dolphins process information, and so too does the human eye and the dolphin eye, but an eye taken by itself does not think. Some creatures, even when complete, seem too simple to be thinking. Presumably an oyster can process information about the sea and the rock but it is not easy to believe that it thinks about these things. Even having a brain doesn't guarantee thought. Fish have brains, but do they think? I doubt whether we know the answer to that question. Then again, the amount of thought that goes with human information-processing varies a great deal. When students listen to lectures and take notes, or read books and write essays, they sometimes think and sometimes don't. Some students seem able to listen carefully and take careful notes without understanding much or anything of what the lecturer says. Some students seem able to skim through books and make reasonably coherent notes without having a clue as to what the books are saying. Listening accompanied by automatic note-taking, and reading followed by mindless plagiarism, are good examples of processing information, though not examples of good work.

Language and Language Rules

One difference between mice and oysters on the one hand, and human beings and computers on the other, is that the mice and oysters do not have language (as far as we know) whereas computers and human beings do. But in spite of the fact that computers deal with codes and languages it is commonly said that they do not really think because they have syntax without semantics. What this slogan means is that computers use linguistic rules but don't know the meanings, the contents, of the strings of symbols which the rules generate.

Does this matter? Perhaps understanding content is not a necessary component in the use and understanding of language. Perhaps some human thinking is purely syntactical. If purely syntactical exercises are ever carried out by human beings, and if they then count as one kind of thinking, then computers too can think. (In *Grundgesetze* (vol. 2 section 90) Frege remarks that someone might follow rules in constructing formulae, and so write proofs, without having a clue as to what it all meant.)

The idea that communication depends on rules is quite important but it has often been over-emphasized. Communication requires first and foremost something to be communicated. It also requires a someone or a something in the set-up who understands the content of the communiqué.

Why don't computers have thoughts with content? Machines as we know them have no understanding of content because there is no place or way for that particular function to enter the system directly. Consider concrete nouns. Each noun has its own sense (or senses) stemming from connections between the word and the world. Human thinking first sets up, and then depends upon, connections between words and things. When it is said that computers have no semantics, part of what is meant, I suppose, is that computers are incapable of either seeing, or setting up, the connections between words and things.

Now it might be thought that the incapacity is due to the fact that computer outputs (words on a screen, for example) are caused by inputs consisting of physical phenomena (electrical impulses) which themselves have no representational function. But that cannot be the explanation. The question as to how merely physical inputs can eventuate in representation of content has not yet been explained, as far as I know, but it is certain that such inputs do result in representation of content because it is certain that this actually occurs in the case of the human brain. What goes into the human head, the input, is a lot of photons and sound waves and so on, which in themselves are mere physical phenomena, while much of the output is language and thoughts.

One huge difference between the computer and the brain is that the first (merely physical) inputs into human thinking are non- or pre-symbolic, whereas with a computer all inputs, including the earliest, already have representational roles, i.e., roles which *for us* are representational. Computers operate with symbols, that is, with physical things or marks or events which have already been given content *by us and for us*. The semantic function, the content, enters the system indirectly, via the human designer. But in the case of the brain the function enters the system directly, it comes straight off the world, as it were.

Causal chains of object–perception–belief are the beginnings of human thinking and the beginnings of any other animal thinking that there might be on our planet. If you should happen to truly believe that there is a dead rat in the vicinity that is either because you have been told so in words (symbols), or because you have seen or smelt something. In the latter case the input comes directly off the world. *Qua* input it is pre- or non-symbolic (it is a smell, for instance). True, the expression 'dead rat' means something, and means what it does mean, partly because of its role in the language as a union of adjective and noun, partly because of the conventions that attach the particular words 'deceased' and 'rat' to these and those kinds of things, and partly because we use all words in rule-following ways. Nevertheless the history of how the expression got its meaning does not start with linguistic rules. The rules themselves arose from pre-meaning encounters between human beings equipped with eyes and brains and noses (on the one hand) and material objects in various states of florescence and decay (on the other).

In our world material things and their visible states not only govern the meanings of (many) words, they are also needed to initiate meanings. How, in our world, could things possibly be otherwise? The set-up which lies behind the computer's production of the marks 'dead rat' is quite different. The computer did not start off by having a rat's body waved in front of its screen or jammed into its disc slot. The marks, the words, get into the computer's software but the object itself has no role.

Varieties of Thought

Human thinking is very various. Its species include (i) accurate or inaccurate mental input (perception, memory), (ii) poor or successful processing of information (reproducing, judging, calculating), and (iii) wise or unwise mental output (deciding, willing, planning). These major species of thinking belong to the intellectual aspect of mental life. Other species or aspects – such as fear, hope, expectation – do not fit neatly into the three categories just mentioned.

Wittgenstein argues that human thinking has no single essential feature but is a collection of processes, states and dispositions such as hoping, day-dreaming, imagining, predicting, concentration, worry, fear, belief and expectation. To suppose that thinking is just one thing is like supposing that athletics is only one thing – sprinting for instance – whereas athletics in fact includes hurdling and weight-lifting and archery and pole-vaulting and many other activities.

The comparison, however, is not helpful for those who wish to argue that computers do not think. Even though sprinting isn't the only kind of athletic activity, still, sprinters are athletes and by parallel reasoning we might say that, although human thinking has many forms, each form taken separately counts as thinking. So it could be argued that if a computer can do at least one of the things that count as human thinking then it too can think.

Computers do process information but in human beings the processing of information is *only one* of at least three species of *only one* aspect of thinking. The significance of this is that only a holistic theory which allows for connections between the varieties of thought can give an adequate account of human (paradigm) thinking.

Three Kinds of Holism

Human thinking, as Schopenhauer says, has a biological function. Man is an animal and animal thinking has a natural evolutionary history. Thus human thinking is holistic in the sense that it is an integral part of the natural life of human beings. The situation is quite otherwise with computers. The behaviour of a computer has no natural evolutionary history because the computer itself has no natural evolutionary history. The behaviour of a computer has no biological function because the computer is not a biological entity. Depriving a computer of its floppy discs will not upset it or make it ill or shorten its existence. Machine behaviour isn't dedicated to promoting the survival of the machine. Computers are not alive and they have no desires and so they cannot possibly be dominated by the will to live.

Thought is not only biologically holistic, it is also logically holistic, and causally holistic. We saw how Wittgenstein says that thinking comprises a collection of states and processes, yet even he does not suggest that thought is a ragbag. He speaks of family resemblances between different kinds of thinking and he describes some of the logical connections that hold between different states of mind.

Thinking is logically holistic in that there are necessary connections between many of its different varieties. Here are some examples. Beliefs entail other beliefs, of course, but so do emotions and intentions and expectations. Fear of failure, for instance, entails a belief that failure is possible. Decisions entail at least a few true or false beliefs about what is feasible and what is not. Gratitude entails belief in the existence of a benefactor, known or even unknown (W. E. Henley: 'I thank whatever gods may be . . .'). Resentment entails a belief that you've been injured. And one's expectations might well entail a belief in astrology, or in Newton's laws, or in a principle of induction. In short it is not possible to be in states of mind such as fear, resentment, gratitude, expectation, hope and so on without also having beliefs.

Thinking is causally holistic because for every individual there will be many psychological connections between mental states of different types. Thus particular desires can produce particular intentions and particular beliefs can lead to particular wishes. In some people a wish that something or other be true will induce the belief that it *is* true.

Because human thinking is logically and causally holistic it is doubly impossible for a human being to be a believer and nothing else, or an intender and nothing else, or a resenter and nothing else, or a rememberer, planner, lover, hater, hoper, expecter and nothing else. The functions of computers, on the other hand, are not elements in suchlike networks. If (which is absurd) machines had beliefs and intentions those beliefs and intentions, so-called, would be truncated items. Machines lack the desires and instincts and emotions which are the product of evolution. The states of machines lack the logical connections that knit together beliefs and other human mental states. And although machine-states have electrical connections (of course), these could not mimic the links between human beliefs and desires and emotions because machines don't have any desires and emotions in the first place.

In people the network of connected beliefs and desires and intentions and emotions is immensely complicated. I surmise that the real reason why some folk deny that the other animals can think is the obscurely recognized fact that in other animals the networks are simpler than those in the human animal. It's not that other creatures have no beliefs or memories or emotions, on the contrary, it is very obvious that all the higher animals do. Their networks are simpler because animals, or anyway those we are most familiar with (dogs, cats, horses, cage birds), have fewer beliefs and plans than we do. They have fewer beliefs because they have less knowledge, and they have fewer plans and intentions, either because they do not measure time, or (perhaps) because their awareness of time and times is a lot less complicated than ours is. Their simpler networks are quantitatively different from ours but probably qualitatively similar. Their mental functions are holistic.

Conclusions

There are many kinds of human thinking. If each type counted as thinking, even when taken alone, then there is a case, but only a *prima facie* case, that computers can think.

Not all information-processing requires thought or understanding. Students, for example, can process information without understanding it.

Computer thought is unlike human thought because it is contentless, and it is contentless because it has no direct connection with the non-human natural world. There are fundamental connections between human language and its meanings, and the natural world. For human beings the natural world has two semantic roles. First, it initiates meaning in general. Second, in many cases it governs particular meanings. In the case of computers both these natural-world roles are filled by a human designer who already possesses language.

Human thinking is holistic – in three ways – and computer thinking is not. The mental activity of higher animals, though simpler than the human, is presumably holistic and in that way is closer to our human thinking than are the operations of computers.

There are thus big gulfs between human thinking and computer thinking. These gulfs are so wide that the word thinking when used of computers can only be a metaphor.

Yet metaphorical meanings sometimes supplant literal ones and become literal themselves. In a hundred years' time, as Turing hinted, people might say and believe that it is machines, and not human beings, which really think. If that state of affairs comes about it might become difficult to hang onto the respect for human life which is the foundation of moral thinking in general and of democratic social concepts in particular.

PART THREE

Deaths and Lives

CHAPTER SEVEN

Euthanasia – For and Against

> 'We desperately need a thorough-going defence of the weak, the
> poor and of life itself.'
>
> David Alton MP, 1995

Euthanasia is defined in the *Oxford English Dictionary* as 'a gentle
and easy death; bringing about of this, esp. in case of incurable
and painful disease'. Another name for bringing about an easy
death is mercy killing. It occurs in wartime when soldiers or
civilians undergoing terrible suffering from burns or wounds or
nerve gas are shot by friends (or by enemies). In peacetime mercy
killing is usually carried out by medical practitioners.

The word euthanasia is also used, euphemistically, to describe
practices and motives which have little to do with mercy. Thus
infanticide both ancient and modern has been so described because deformed infants are amongst those killed. This usage tends
to blur the fact that throughout recorded history most infants
killed at birth have been, not deformed, but female. Secondly, it
happens now and then that financial considerations in favour of
'euthanasia' are hinted at (or even openly mentioned) by managers of National Health Service hospitals in Britain and politicians
in Australia. Again, this use of the word has nothing to do with
mercy. Thirdly, supporters of Social Darwinism, or eugenics,
occasionally speak of the destruction of supposedly inferior infants as euthanasia. Social Darwinism used to be quite a popular
creed with Western intellectuals before the Second World War
but the revelation, in 1945, of the genocidal atrocities resulting
from Nazi eugenic theory led to a temporary revulsion against
such ideas. Nevertheless the dream (or nightmare) of trying to

improve the human race, either by controlled breeding or by legalizing selective 'euthanasia' and selective abortion, seems to have enduring fascination.

We see, then, that proposals to legalize mercy killing are tangled up with considerations unrelated to mercy. These tangles will be ignored until we reach the final section of the following chapter (chapter 8). I will also try to ignore the really feeble reasons given in favour of euthanasia, though it is necessary to mention one feeble reason because in spite of its weakness it is popular and influential. This is the grotesque argument: 'It's happening already so let's legalize it.' The grotesqueness of the reasoning is easy to see once we realize that it is not applied to crimes against property (even minor ones like shoplifting) nor in general to blue-collar crimes. In the present context it has to do with the alleged behaviour of doctors and nurses – educated, middle-class, professional people. It is an argument which secretly and silently distinguishes between citizens of different social status and is therefore in conflict with natural justice.

From this point on I will be discussing euthanasia in the proper sense of the word, the sense in which it means death brought about solely for the good, or at the very least for the supposed good, of the person who dies.

Voluntary, Non-voluntary and Involuntary Euthanasia

Philosophy teachers and others have given labels to different kinds of mercy killing. The labels are not very accurate but I will use them all the same because they are familiar.

Voluntary euthanasia is the label given to deaths which are asked for by people who are then 'helped to die'. Such individuals presumably find that suicide is for some reason difficult or even impossible.

There is disagreement as to when the request has to be made.

Euthanasia – For and Against

In the USA supporters of euthanasia have argued that the law ought to recognize living wills, that is to say, written statements in which individuals ask either to be allowed to die, or to be actually put to death, should certain eventualities arise. These eventualities might include disabling stroke or coma caused by head injuries. The possible validation of living wills is a contentious matter, partly because of the assumption that such wills can ask only for death and not for life. The euthanasia lobby does not seem to think that written demands to be kept alive for as long as possible ought to be recognized in law.

Non-voluntary euthanasia means a death which is not asked for because the the patient is either unconscious or too young to speak. In such cases it is argued that the individual would ask to die if he or she could express any wishes.

Involuntary euthanasia is the label given to the killing of conscious patients who have not been consulted about the matter. Virtually all utilitarian philosophy teachers argue in favour of involuntary euthanasia in certain circumstances. One kind of case concerns terminally ill children who are conscious and old enough to speak. It is claimed that the parents of such children should be allowed to decide for them. Another example is that of people suffering from senile decay and incapable of rational judgement. It is argued that their families, if any, or the medical profession, should be allowed to decide for them.

Seven different reasons can be given in support of mercy killing. These are: 1) a philosophical thesis, namely, that every rational person has an inalienable and unrestricted right to suicide; 2) an assumption about ownership – the assumption that one's life is one's own; 3) a material fact, viz., the fact that some diseases are extremely painful; 4) a judgement to the effect that some lives, even if not subject to much pain, are nevertheless not worth living; 5) the opinion that it is degrading and undignified to be dependent on others for care; 6) the idea that modern medical techniques force us to accept mercy killing in many cases; and 7) a philosophical theory about acts and omissions.

Autonomy

A popular argument in favour of (voluntary) euthanasia rests on a dictum about autonomy: in all choices which concern only one particular individual that individual's wishes must be treated as paramount.

Campaigners for the legalization of euthanasia say that the quintessence of voluntary euthanasia is personal choice and self-control 'with sometimes a little help from one's friends'. One such campaigner appealing to a respect for autonomy defines the principle thus: '[it] tells us to allow rational agents to live their own lives according to their own autonomous decisions, free from coercion or interference; but if rational agents should autonomously choose to die then respect for autonomy will lead us to assist them to do as they choose'.

There is plainly something wrong with this reasoning. The principle of autonomy as described above would allow doctors to kill anyone, including young healthy people, on request. For why should only sick people be given autonomy in this matter?

One version of the principle just referred to comes to us from Kant. The versions to be found in the works of modern thinkers, however, are not always variations that Kant himself would have recognized. Utilitarian philosophers speak and write as if autonomy was nothing more nor less than a stark form of self-determination. J. S. Mill held that there is a universal right to live or die as one wishes provided one doesn't harm anyone else. However, modern utilitarians defending euthanasia usually concentrate on sick people and do not discuss the autonomy of the healthy.

Kant, who of course was not a utilitarian, regards autonomy as a *precondition* of morality. For him it is both a moral entitlement and a moral foundation, hence the Kantian right to autonomy is not the same thing as a right to have one's (seemingly) rational self-regarding desires treated as absolutely paramount. Moreover, it is well known that Kant believes suicide to be a violation of the moral law and therefore essentially irrational. He would reject the casual assumption that the wish to die is or can be just as rational as any other desire. Medical practice follows Kant in this matter. In cases of attempted suicide the will of the individual is certainly not treated as paramount, for it is normal practice for doctors and ambulance workers to revive would-be suicides if they can.

Is it true that self-destruction is always irrational? That it is often irrational is obvious since many suicides take place as the result of drugs or depression while some of those who commit the deed are just weak or weak-minded or cowardly or psychologically unable to take long-term views. In such cases we may well feel that the will itself is as it were diseased. On the other hand, Kant's attempt to prove that suicide is necessarily irrational is somewhat less convincing than his parallel claim that a man who makes lying promises is necessarily irrational.

It seems to me that there is room for rational autonomy even in the extreme case of self-destruction. But there is not much room. The instinct for survival is very strong and its apparent absence is a *prima facie* reason to conclude that the individual is not thinking rationally.

Even in the comparatively rare cases in which the wish for death seems to be rational it should not be assumed that it is reasonable to ask another person to kill. Suppose a completely sane individual is nearing death and wishes to die more quickly than would happen in the normal course of events. Suppose that this individual is bedridden and in hospital and believes he lacks the wherewithal to kill himself. Should his doctor be asked to speed the death? Suppose the doctor doesn't like killing people? Suppose the doctor believes it is wrong to kill? Has the patient any right to demand that the doctor kills? Shouldn't the autonomy of the physician be respected too? After all, even a bedridden person can refuse food and refusing food, especially if one is already seriously ill, soon ends in death. Moreover lack of food, unlike lack of liquids, does not cause severe distress – or so we learn from the reported experiences of the suffragettes and other hunger-strikers.

This incidentally raises questions about the morality of force-feeding. Although doctors should do their best to persuade unhappy patients to take nourishment there might come a point when only compulsory feeding will work. Now it seems clear that medical treatment ought not be *compulsory*. Most people think it was wrong to force-feed the suffragettes. To my mind it is wrong to force-feed anyone at all. On the other hand drip-feeding an unconscious person isn't the same thing as force-feeding; it is more akin to reviving someone who can't be asked what he wants.

Ownership

The popular question or slogan 'whose life is it anyway?' seems to suggest that each person owns his or her own life. It suggests that life is a kind of property.

It might be retorted that individual human lives belong at least in part to the community – this view of the matter was taken by certain ancient peoples. Still, let us suppose, for the sake of argument, that I do own my own life. Does it follow that I should be allowed to destroy myself? The right to destroy a trifling possession, like a newspaper or a cup and saucer, need not be questioned but that doesn't mean that one may rightly destroy anything at all which one happens to own. It is questionable whether ownership confers an absolute right to destroy things which are valuable or unique. If I was the legal owner of a wonderful collection of works of art would many art lovers agree that I had a right to destroy it? If I was the legal owner of the last pair of peregrine falcons in the whole world should I be allowed to kill them?

The notion of 'owning' one's life is in any case rather peculiar. We speak of 'my' life and 'your' life but that doesn't necessarily imply genuine ownership. After all, I can speak of *my* uncle and *my* aunts, and so on, but that doesn't mean that I own my uncles and aunts and nephews, etc. It would be preposterous to argue that I may kill my uncle just because he is my uncle, preposterous to ask, rhetorically, 'whose uncle is it anyway?' in defence of such a murder. In other words not all uses of the possessive pronouns my, yours, and so on, imply a property right.

Pain

The fear of incurable pain is probably the main reason why many ordinary folk support the idea of mercy killing. People say: 'We wouldn't treat a dog like that! When dogs are in pain they are put out of their misery and we should do the same for human beings.' But it is dangerous to draw analogies between the treatment of human beings and the treatment of the other animals. It was suggested in chapter 5 that the result, in practice, of blurring the differences between human beings and the other animals is to reduce respect for the former without necessarily increasing respect for the latter. When people in the past treated human beings as animals the outcomes were dreadful. Farmers brand horses and cows; white Americans used to brand their black slaves. Ordinary common sense suggests that we should try to learn from the past and the past teaches us that a failure to differentiate between human beings and other creatures can have results quite different from those expected by philosophy teachers.

In recent discussions on British radio and TV, and in newspapers, some doctors said that people suffering severe and incurable pain should be 'helped to die'. Other physicians replied that modern methods of pain control are so successful that the supposed need to end lives because of pain has been removed. In this debate the medicos in favour of euthanasia seemed to be general practitioners whereas the anti-euthanasia doctors were consultants specializing in pain control and palliative care.

It has been said that 'euthanasia is the last resort of the thera-

71

peutically destitute', the last resort, that is, of doctors who are not aware of all the possibilities for pain control.

In its evidence to the House of Lords Select Committee on Euthanasia the Association of Palliative Medicine stated that in most patients it is now possible to control the pain and other distressing symptoms of terminal cancer. The Select Committee accepted the following definition of palliative care:

> [It] is delivered by a health care team and concentrates on the quality of life and alleviation of pain and other distressing symptoms. It aims neither to hasten nor to postpone death.

In Britain palliative medicine is practised in hospices for the dying and also, in some areas, in patients' homes.

The hospice movement came into being at a time when fear of cancer was almost universal. Advances in palliative medicine together with an increasing public awareness of hospices have 'won the battle against cancer'. Supporters of euthanasia no longer think of sufferers from this particular disease as being typical of those in need of mercy killing. They are more likely, these days, to mention AIDS.

Some of those who oppose the principles of palliative care do so because they believe that a modern hospital system cannot cope with the dying: there are too many of them! Others believe that it is a waste of money looking after people who are not going to be cured. (This is an attitude of the healthy and tends to change as the healthy grow older.) In fact palliative care is not a very expensive form of medical treatment.

Dr James Gilbert MRCP, of the Exeter Hospice, writes as follows:

> Palliative care affirms life and regards death as a normal process – neither hastens nor postpones death – offers a support system to help patients live as actively as possible until death – offers a support system to help those close to the patient to cope both during the patient's illness and in their own bereavement.

He goes on to describe the clinical activity of the charity Hospiscare which provides specialist palliative treatment for a population of about 300,000 in the south-west of England. The treatment of the dying in the area consists of a mixture of homecare, daycare, in-patient care, out-patient consultation and hospital support and reaches (annually) 700 of the 1,000 local cancer patients and about 30 people with other incurable diseases. The cost is estimated at approximately £6 per head per annum for the 300,000 people in the district. Dr Gilbert says:

> The hospice experience of the last three decades is that when high quality care of this type is provided to those with advanced progressive diseases the demand for euthanasia on grounds of compassion disappears.

Quality of Life

An argument commonly adduced in support of non-voluntary and involuntary euthanasia has to do with 'poor quality of life'. Examples frequently mentioned include the lives of babies born with the deformity of spina bifida or with milder defects such as Down's syndrome or haemophilia, the lives of people in coma, and the lives of people suffering from Alzheimer's disease.

It will be noticed that non-voluntary and involuntary euthanasia cannot be defended by appeals to autonomy. In both non-voluntary and involuntary euthanasia it is presupposed that the subject is for one reason or another unable to exercise autonomy at all. In other words the decision is taken by someone other than the patient. To have someone else decide that your life is not worth living is not compatible with autonomy.

There is no doubt that some lives are in some sense better than others. The lives of gaolbirds and drug addicts do not have much to recommend them whereas the lives of actors (say), or nurses, or fond parents of clever happy children, or even Lord Mayors, are, or can be, good in lots of different ways. The crucial question is not: Which lives are good, which bad? But: Are there any lives of which it can be judged, by outsiders, and with certainty, that *they are not worth living at all*?

The answer to this question has to be No. First, because what counts as good or bad quality of life varies according to which outsider happens to be making the judgement. Thus some supporters of non-voluntary euthanasia believe that to lose one's reason is to lose all quality of life, others hold that quality of life disappears when one loses certain physical capacities like the ability to feed oneself, and yet others try to put together a basket of mental and physical characteristics which, they claim, make up a minimally good life. Secondly, it is not only those, or even mostly those, whose lives have been described, by outsiders, as not worth living, who commit suicide. Severely crippled people, for example, do not necessarily wish to die: in Britain (according to news reports) people serving long terms of imprisonment commit suicide less frequently than prisoners on remand, and only some kinds of mental illness involve proneness to self-destruction. The people incarcerated, effectively for life, in Stalin's labour camps seemed to want to go on living. In spite of the message propagated by the play and film *Whose Life Is It Anyway?* it is not impossible for people in iron lungs to want to go on living.

It has already been argued in an earlier chapter that the judgement that a life is not worth living cannot be made from outside. When judged from inside virtually every type of human life turns out to be worth living for many or most of those who are living it. It follows that there is always reason to believe that a judgement to the effect that some other person's life is not worth living will not only be inconsistent with autonomy but all too often a violation of autonomy.

Dignity and Degradation

Is it degrading to be dependent on others for care? Is caring a degradation for the carers?

Caring for other people is a natural human activity. To say that an activity is natural does not mean that everyone is or could be engaged in it. Natural human activities are exceedingly various and no one individual could be natural in all the different ways there are of being natural in a single lifetime. It is natural for human beings to join together in groups, and to give parties, and eat and drink and dance together. It is also natural for them to choose to live alone. It is natural for human beings to express their joys and sorrows but also natural to be reticent about those things. It is natural (as Aristotle said) for human beings to engage in politics but not everyone wants to be a professional politician. *Natural for human beings* is a many-track concept, not a single-track one.

How do we know that caring and being cared for are natural and not unnatural? Well, every human society has situations in which people care for one another. Parents care for children, young people care for older people, and wherever the practice of medicine exists – be it scientific and successful or primitive and chancy – there will be doctors (or witch doctors) who care for their patients. If it is degrading to be dependent on others then everyone is degraded at some point.

Is it degrading to care for others? Surely not. Caring for others is an important human trait which can given meaning to individual lives. Disillusioned young people in the wealthy West find meaning in helping sick people in Africa and India or impoverished people in their own home towns. Finally, the view that caring for others is degrading is an idea that itself degrades the whole medical profession.

Modern Medical Techniques

It is sometimes argued that modern medical techniques have produced situations which demand a 'new morality'. The reasoning begins from the fact that modern techniques can keep patients alive, for a long time, on life-support machines. Because intensive care keeps patients alive who would otherwise die it can come about that people who will never recover to the point at which they regain consciousness can be kept alive indefinitely. Doctors need to make judgements which were once unknown, judgements about who to place on life support in the first place, and, later, judgements about when to switch the machine off. Because these judgements are in a sense new, some philosophy teachers say that a 'new ethics' is needed to answer the 'new' questions. But there is no more reason to want a 'new' ethics here than there was when the cause of malaria was discovered, or when penicillin, or vaccines, were discovered. We just need to take new and more careful thought about the 'old' ethics.

Life-support machines are very expensive. The training, and the salaries, of the nurses who work in intensive care units are also very costly. These facts are adduced by utilitarian philosophy professors as reasons for switching off the machines. But since cost is also a reason for not installing the machines in the first place we must ignore it as irrelevant.

We need to understand, or rather to remind ourselves, what exactly intensive care is for. What are life-support machines, why are they used? What is their purpose?

Dr J. F. Searle writes as follows:

The purpose of intensive care is to provide monitoring and organ support for patients with critical illnesses from which recovery is possible. Despite increasing technological and pharmacological sophistication mortality in intensive care units remains high with significant disability in those who survive.

Methods of predicting outcome from intensive care have been developed. These enable patients to be placed in risk groups but do not accurately predict the outcome of individual patients. That prediction is a clinical judgement based on the underlying disease, the number of body systems failing and the length of time for which intensive care support has been necessary.

Once a decision has been made to withhold or withdraw intensive care the principles of good palliative medicine should be employed during what will then be the inevitable terminal phase of the illness.

The purpose of intensive care is not different from the purpose of prescribing antibiotic drugs: it is *to cure the patient*. A fever victim is cured when his fever is permanently dispelled and a coma victim is cured when he comes out of his coma. Whether or not the patient in intensive care *can* be cured is not easy to predict. Dr Searle reports that the recovery rate varies a great deal from one IC unit to another and also between different types of patient. People predicted to die sometimes live, those predicted to live often die. But in spite of all that the purpose of treatment is what it always is: to cure the patient. If in a particular case it becomes clear that the IC treatment is merely drawing out the process of dying, merely making the death process longer than it would otherwise be, then the treatment has failed, it has turned out to unsuccessful.

It is not necessary or sensible to try to redefine death; nor is it reasonable to speak of a 'new ethics'. For we do not need a 'new ethics' to tell us that curing a patient is not the same thing as prolonging his death. The philosophy teachers who argue that a 'new ethics' is needed here do so because they have an inadequate understanding of what it is to kill. The question of what it is to kill will be discussed in the next chapter.

CHAPTER EIGHT

Euthanasia – Logic and Practice

'If life were a guerdon that money could buy
The rich they would live and the poor they would die'

Old proverb

Acts and Omissions

Euthanasia is sometimes classified as passive or active. The passive kind is said to occur when medical treatment is either not started or is brought to an end – this is called an omission. Active euthanasia is said to occur when someone carries out some deed, such as administering a lethal drug, with the intention of quickly ending the patient's life – this is called an action.

The role of the act–omission distinction in modern philosophy is dubious since many people deny its very existence; this, indeed, is one of the orthodoxies of contemporary thought. Philosophy teachers argue that there is no moral difference between active and passive euthanasia because they reject the supposed principle that there is a universal and inherent moral difference between acts and omissions. Yet the supposed principle or distinction seems to be something of a straw man. Although it is often attacked, no one seems to know who, if anyone, has ever believed it. That there is *sometimes* a moral difference between an act and an omission is a perfectly rational view.

What are actions and omissions? It is tempting to think that an action is essentially a bodily movement (like lifting one's arm) and that an omission is a sort of sitting still. Indeed, lifting one's arm is very often taken, by philosophy teachers, to be a paradigm action, an ideal case. However, this alleged paradigm gives an impoverished view of actions and activities. Some actions involve no overt physical movements. Many actions include purpose as well as locatable movement.

It is better to define actions and activities as: *items which can be meaningfully mentioned in answering the questions 'What are you doing? What are they doing? (etc.).'* Some possible answers are: They are lifting their arms. They are voting. He is showing the doctor that he can lift his arm. He is waving goodbye. I am getting rid of a bee on my hand. I am warning someone. Other possible answers are: I am doing mental arithmetic. He is composing a poem. They are waiting for Godot.

As to omissions, the best way to understand them is to see them as parasitic on what is omitted. In many cases an omission will indeed consist of the not-doing of a physical movement. It can also consist in stopping something – giving up waiting for Godot for instance. But these are not the only kinds of case because one can omit an omission (as it were). Here is an example (adapted from Wittgenstein). You start counting in two's, that is, as you count you omit all the odd numbers. Then you omit to omit one of the odd numbers, say 9. In other words your counting goes like this: 2 4 6 8 9 10 12 14 . . .

Omissions are parasitic on actions, or activities, or on other omissions, because reference to an omission implies that some action, or activity, or some other omission, is *expected*. Omissions occur when one fails to do something which would be according to a rule which one is following (as in the counting example above). Or when one fails to do something that needs to be done as part of an activity one is engaged in; or fails to do something which belongs to the execution of one's plan or purpose; or fails to perform a task for which one has been paid; or fails to do something for which one has accepted responsibility. Then again, an omission can occur because one has failed to live up to ordinary standards of human decency, or to one's own standards of decency.

The question as to whether acts as such and omissions as such are similar or different has no answer because it is not a sensible question in the first place. You might as well ask whether twelve and half are similar or different types of number. There is no answer to this question because half, taken alone, is not a number at all. Of course half OF (12 or 20 or 30 or . . .) is a number. In much the same way omissions have to be omissions OF something. They are not simply passive not-doings but failures to perform the expected or the needed. To repeat: an omission occurs when you fail to perform something promised: or something contracted: or the next move in a game: or a move (or omission) in a rule-following situation: or an act of ordinary decency; and so on. It follows that the simple not-doing of something that might have had good results is not an omission at all, strictly speaking. However, if one knows about the possible good results it might in some circumstances count as an omission under the ordinary decency rubric. More generally, failing to do what is expected or rational or owed *can* be morally bad.

According to basic utilitarian theory the goodness or badness of human behaviour is connected directly to consequences. Thus contemporary utilitarian philosophy teachers have argued that not giving money to charity is just as wicked as killing people 'whenever the two courses of conduct result in an equal number of deaths'. Philippa Foot, on the other hand, insists that failing to give money to Oxfam cannot be as wicked as sending poisoned food to refugee camps. And surely she is right.

Let us agree that *some* failures to act are just as bad as positive actions. It does not follow that their badness is due solely to their consequences. Consequences are relevant in moral judgement but so are other matters.

To my mind the following example (borrowed from Elizabeth Anscombe) proves conclusively that consequences alone cannot determine what is good and bad in actions and omissions.

80

If omitting an action which would save a life really was, in all cases, as bad as killing someone, them omitting an action which would kill would be, in all cases, as good as saving a life. Now, saving a life is usually regarded as a deed which deserves praise. Since my failure to kill my neighbours goes on every day and every minute of the day the praise I deserve, if this 'omission' really deserved praise, would be enormous. But that idea is ludicrous.

If the failure to do something which would have bad results does not always deserve praise we have no reason to think that failure to do something that would have good results always deserves blame. Still, we have agreed that some failures to act are just as good or as bad as positive deeds. So we need to ask when and why a failure can be just as bad as an action.

Apart from consequences, the things that are relevant to the goodness or badness of human behaviour are: intention; knowledge; skill; difficulty; responsibility; and certain facts about time.

Failing to act can make one guilty of a death but for that to be the case one must know what is going on. If you walk past a river in which someone is drowing but do not hear his shrieks you can't later be accused of his death. If you do hear him but don't try to save him then the difficulty of the action, or your own weakness or incompetence, can make a difference.

On the other hand if you let someone drown when you know what is happening and could easily save him then you certainly fail to do what human decency demands. Are you then a murderer? Well, even if your behaviour is just as bad as murder that doesn't necessarily mean it *is* murder. Not everything that is bad is bad in the same way or for the same reason. Omitting to save him when it would have been easy to do so makes you guilty of his death, but we needn't leap to the conclusion that the omission was actually murder.

If one has special responsibilities then not doing something can in certain circumstances be just as bad as positively doing some-

81

thing and might even be the same kind of thing. Suppose it is decided that a certain man's life can only be saved by putting him onto a life-support machine. Suppose that the doctor or nurse in charge fails to connect the patient to the machine. Here the fact that the medical worker has accepted responsibility for connecting the machine makes a huge difference to the character of the omission. The whole point of using the machine, the whole point of making the connection, was to save the patient's life; hence if someone with responsibility deliberately fails to make the connection the omission is not just like a murder, it is murder.

The way time makes a difference is to be seen in the fact that the answer to the question: When did you kill? is always different from the answer to: When did you fail to kill? It is possible to kill quickly or slowly but in either case the act has to occur at a specific time, that is to say, either at a specific moment or over a specific period. Failing to kill occurs over an unspecific period, it goes on continually (as it were). During that unspecific period you *could* kill but you didn't: you remain merely capable of becoming a killer. Having the capacity to kill is obviously not the same thing as being a killer.

Logic

Some philosophy teachers seem to believe it is illogical to distinguish between allowing to die and helping to die (i.e., killing). This is a piece of 'logic' which no logician could accept. There is no inconsistency in saying that (i) when a doctor has no obligation to prolong treatment it is (ii) also the case that he must not kill his patient.

The technical (logical) reasons are as follows. First, saving and killing are not opposites, they are not contradictories but merely contraries. Hence not-saving is not equivalent to killing. Secondly, killing and treating are not even contraries; logically they

82

are wholly independent. Hence not-treating is not equivalent to killing.*

Given that killing and discontinuing (or not starting) treatment are logically independent of one another we must try to find a common-sense answer to the question: When might it be right to stop or not start treatment usually thought of as life-saving?

First: ought implies can. In many parts of the world there are no life-support machines. It is self-evident that there can be no obligation to give treatment if the wherewithal is unavailable.

Next: there is no obligation to try to save someone who is already dead; this too is self-evident! The issue is complicated by a current diversity of medical definitions of death (which won't be discussed here).

Third: in certain situations it becomes clear, after a time, that a person will die unless repeatedly and endlessly resuscitated. At some point the resuscitation changes character, it ceases to be a life-saving operation and becomes a prolongation of the process of dying. At that point the obligation to continue presumably ends.

Fourth: there cannot be any obligation to give treatment which has very dangerous side-effects or which might kill the patient. Doubtless there are borderline cases requiring much professional skill and judgement. Here, too, there are other obligations – for example there is an obligation to explain the difficulties to the patient (if he or she is conscious) or to the patient's relatives. There could well be an obligation to consult other doctors before deciding what to do.

---

* *Coloured* and *colourless* are contradictories. Nothing can be both those things at once and every material substance has to be either one or the other. *Not-coloured* means exactly the same as *colourless*.

Green and *purple* are contraries. Nothing can be both at once but many things are neither. *Not-green* does not mean the same as *purple*.

Green and *rectangular* are logically independent. So an object can be either or neither or both.

Finally: medical treatment ought not to be compulsory. There is no obligation to force adult or teenage patients to accept treatment absolutely against their will. Some of the 'case histories' described by the pro-euthanasia lobby come from America where the almost limitless possibilities of litigation have produced a situation in which hospitals can feel compelled to more or less force patients to accept treatment. The case against euthanasia, however, is not a case for compulsory treatment. Compulsory treatment is a distortion produced by an accidental feature of a particular legal system.

Very old people sometimes decide that they do not want to endure the hassle or pain of further medical treatment. They might want to go home to die in peace. Provided the decision is serious it seems reasonable that their medical advisors should stop treatment.

Stopping treatment is compatible with respect for the patient and respect for human life. In the various situations described above the action of killing the patient would not be 'just the same kind of thing'.

Living and Dying in the Real World

The euthanasia lobby no doubt contains some well-meaning individuals who sincerely believe that 'helping' very sick people to die is normally an act of kindness. These well-meaning people, alas, are not living in the real world. In their mental lives they inhabit an ideal and purely imaginary universe containing only ideal human beings. Their ideal world contains no sons and daughters, or sons-in-law and daughters-in-law, who fail to love and respect their old folk, no sons and daughters and in-laws capable of putting the old folk into 'Homes' against their will. In the ideal world kith and kin do not have debts that could be easily paid if only Grand-dad would hurry up and die. The ideal world contains doctors and nurses who need no taboos because they are *naturally* more virtuous and noble and intelligent than other people. In the ideal world imagined by well-meaning supporters of euthanasia doctors and nurses never treat patients in a condescending fashion and never get fed up with dirty, troublesome old people. In the ideal world no one at all – no politician, no doctor, no ordinary man in the street – ever distinguishes, even unconsciously, still less consciously, between rich and poor, old and young, male and female, black and white. In the ideal world doctors and nurses never misdescribe the causes of deaths on death certificates and would never break the law. In the ideal world imagined by well-meaning supporters of mercy killing even doctors who have openly confessed to having broken existing laws against euthanasia can be trusted never to break or bend any proposed new laws. In the ideal world no doctors are touchy and over-sensitive to criticism. In the ideal world no doctors take drugs, no nurses are deranged and no nurse has ever killed a child or disconnected a life-support machine in order to attract attention to herself.

Unfortunately the ideal world is a world of dreams. It is not the real world.

Euthanasia is supported by many consequentialist philosophy teachers, yet there are powerful consequentialist objections to allowing the practice. These objections are not visible to thinkers who don't live in the real world.

The unreality of the world inhabited by typical consequentialists can be seen from the way in which they use examples and counter-examples. The use of counter-examples is important in philosophy because it is a good way of testing generalizations. It isn't necessary that the counter-examples should exist in reality, they can be imaginary. In Plato's *Republic*, for instance, Socrates tests a definition of justice (*returning what is owned to its owner*) by constructing an imaginary counter-example about a madman who owns a knife. Now, although imaginary counter-examples can test a generalization it is well known that imaginary 'pro'-examples cannot establish truth. Consequentialists ignore this principle and try to draw positive conclusions from the *imagined* effects of proposed actions. They reason on the basis of speculations about the *possible* results of future events while ignoring ordinary common-sense estimates of probability and hard evidence about actual real-life consequences. Such guesswork about possible futures is not a good basis for moral philosophy and is certainly not superior to hard facts and common sense. If we know anything at all about the possibility of possible futures that knowledge must itself rest on what we know about actualities and on our common-sense estimates of human probabilities.

What are the probabilities here? What is likely to happen if mercy killing is legalized? And what are the facts? What actually happens when mercy killing is legalized?

Doctors now are trained to save lives. If euthanasia is legalized they will presumably also have to be trained to kill. Killing is perhaps not a very difficult skill, but no doubt there are different methods in which medical students would have to be instructed. The instruction, and the new skill, would alter the character of the work to some extent. It would alter the character of the vocation. It is possible that the kind of people choosing to become doctors would then be rather different from those practising medicine now.

Legalization of mercy killing would certainly reduce the feelings of trust that most people have for members of the medical profession. If medical specialisms were developed (voluntary euthanasianism, non-voluntary euthanasianism and involuntary euthanasianism perhaps), their existence, and the identity of the practitioners, might have to be disguised. After all it would be scary, and very bad for those with weak hearts, to see the hospital specialist in involuntary euthanasianism walking through the ward!

If doctors are allowed to kill it is probable that other people (for instance, nurses, social workers and the relatives of patients) will eventually be allowed to do the same. There is an easy slippery slope here. It is not difficult to see how pragmatic or anti-elitist ideas could push society onto that slippery slope. To begin with it is almost certain that people lobbying for euthanasia would start to argue in favour of expanding the right to 'help people to die'. Laymen would point out that killing does not actually require any very special medical skills. They will ask: why insist that mercy killing be carried out only by highly trained people?

There are other slippery slopes here too. Legalizing euthanasia is virtually certain to make ordinary murder much easier to disguise than it is at present.

Holland and Australia

So much for probabilities. What happens in the real world when voluntary euthanasia is made legal? One thing that happens is an insidious slide from voluntary to involuntary. Philosophy teachers tend to be whole-hoggers in this as in other areas, hence those who support euthanasia commonly argue in favour of all three varieties: non-voluntary and involuntary as well as voluntary. Politicians, on the other hand, usually insist that they wish only to legalize voluntary euthanasia. But they soon let the cat out of the bag, as it were, by mentioning the shortage of hospital beds, the increasing number of old people 'taking up space' on the planet, and the tax burdens of middle-aged middle-income earners. These circumstances, as we have already noted, have nothing to do with mercy.

Laws or practices which allow euthanasia have been introduced in two countries in the West: Holland, and the Northern Territory of Australia. (Unsuccessful attempts to legalize the practice occurred recently in Oregon, USA, and in New Zealand. Oregon's proposed law was struck down by a Federal judge as unconstitutional; the case has gone to appeal. In New Zealand legislation was abandoned after protests from the Maori people.)

In 1992 Brian Pollard, a Fellow of the Faculty of Anaesthetists in the Royal Australasian College of Surgeons, published a study on the effects, in Holland, of the *de facto* legalization of euthanasia.

Article 293 of the Dutch penal code provides a maximum of 12 years' imprisonment for taking the life of another person at that person's 'express and serious request'. In other words, according to the penal code voluntary euthanasia is illegal in Holland. However, in 1984 the Dutch Supreme Court ruled that a doctor was entitled to break the law for the sake of a higher good, the higher good in this case being the relief of severe distress. In 1986 the Court of Appeal in The Hague upheld the ruling of the Supreme Court. Thus the law regarding euthanasia in Holland seems to be that it is legal to break the law. This allows individual doctors enormous discretionary power. (It will be argued in chapter 10 that giving discretionary powers to unelected experts is pretty certain to lead to abuse.) In 1987 the Dutch State Commission on euthanasia recommended that non-voluntary euthanasia should not be an offence if carried out by 'careful' medical practitioners. However, since Article 293 remains on the Statute books, and since no clear directions as to 'when and where' have been given, Dutch doctors who practice euthanasia have a motive for disguising the cause of death when writing death certificates. According to Brian Pollard it is known that medical killing in Holland is practised (at least) 25,000 times a year, representing nearly 20 per cent of all deaths in that country. Of those 25,000 deaths more than half (14,500) are non-voluntary or involuntary. In 1991 a Dutch committee found that 27 per cent of doctors in Holland admitted carrying out euthanasia *without* any requests from the patients. This is the real world.

In Holland 65 per cent of the citizens are now in favour of voluntary and involuntary euthanasia; this could be due to an acceptance of the unsound principle, mentioned earlier in this book, that 'whatever is, is right'. Yet it seems that people quickly change their minds when they themselves become helpless. A Dutch poll taken among patients in nursing homes revealed that 95 per cent were opposed to all forms of euthanasia.

Euthanasia – Logic and Practice

There are over 200 hospices and palliative care units in the UK and fewer than 10 in Holland.

It was partly because of the developments in Holland that the House of Lords Select Committee (1994) rejected the move towards legalizing euthanasia in Britain. The Select Committee recognized the right of every competent person to refuse to consent to medical treatment but judged that allowing voluntary euthanasia would in practice encourage a surreptitious, and probably widespread, use of involuntary euthanasia as well. The lives of many people, especially the elderly, the weak, the impoverised and the inarticulate, would be put at risk. As one commentator observed 'what is voluntary for some soon becomes assumed to be in the best interests of others'.

In Australia's Northern Territory the Bill legalizing euthanasia is called the *Rights of the Terminally Ill Act* but its most novel provisions have to do with the rights and discretionary powers of doctors. The Act, which was passed late at night by 13 votes for to 12 votes against, has a number of interesting Real World features. One Real World feature concerns the area of application. The Northern Territory of Australia is a large and fairly empty state in which about half the population is aboriginal or of mixed race – i.e., black. As far as I know there are no wealthy or highly educated aboriginal blacks in Australia. Until quite recently Australian politicians ignored the native population and its problems altogether. Sympathetic anthropologists were forbidden to enter the Northern Territory, a ban which was not lifted until after the Second World War. In the 1950s the desert area in the south of the Territory, inhabited 'only' by a few nomadic aborigines, was used as a testing ground for the British atomic bomb. The Territory has relatively poor medical services and (as far as I can discover) no state provisions for palliative care. It is possible, of course, that Christian missionaries might be providing some kind of care for the dying.

Another interesting Real World feature is the fact that the Bill removes the authority which professional associations now have to discipline doctors and nurses for breaking association rules.

89

Paragraph 20 of the Act gives immunity from civil or criminal or professional disciplinary action 'for anything done in good faith in compliance with this Act'. Thus once the Act has been promulgated the Australian Medical Association will lose the right and the power to expel or discipline those of its members working in the Northern Territory who decide 'in good faith' to directly kill a patient. Paragraph 20 is a striking example of the way in which bossy governments set out to abolish the independence of professional groups and other spontaneous collections of like-minded citizens. Any government which overrules the traditional regulations whereby the professions and other groups ensure that the behaviour of their members conforms to appropriate standards acts against the long-term interests of its citizens. (The reasons for allowing the professions to impose special ethical standards on their members will be discussed again in chapter 10.)

Although politicians presumably trust doctors to act decently when faced with difficult choices they do not understand *why it is* that doctors can in fact be trusted. Politicians (and other laypeople) seem to think that doctors are trustworthy because doctors have special skills. But that cannot be the whole reason, or even a specially good reason for trust. Many business people have special skills, yet in dealing with businessmen the sensible motto is *caveat emptor* – *let the buyer beware*. The fact that most doctors behave honourably and decently has little to do with their special skills and still less with some imaginary natural virtuousness. It has to do with the fact that the medical profession imposes taboos on itself. These taboos are more than 2,000 years old and have become as it were ingrained in the thinking of doctors almost everywhere. Medical students might or might not get to hear about these taboos but up until now they have learnt them during their training simply by observing the example set by their teachers and by older doctors. In many countries, too, medical students also know that there are professional associations with the power to disbar incompetent and dishonourable practitioners.

The most important of the age-old taboos imposed on physicians is: Do not kill. Politicians and philosophy teachers who wish to get rid of this taboo while at the same time giving individual doctors a discretionary right or duty to end lives are not being very clever.

Although the Northern Territory Act insists, modishly, on rights and autonomy, its political supporters often seem to be interested mainly in getting rid of 'useless old people'. Politicians who support euthanasia speak with surprising brutality, even brutishness. They say that old people 'ought to be dead' because they are 'cluttering up the world'.

When the Australian Medical Association showed signs of objecting to the Northern Territory Act the Chief Minister of the Territory angrily described the distinguished officers of the AMA as 'a lot of dinosaurs'. It would seem that he is not used to having his decisions questioned.

Bill Hayden, Governor-General of Australia, defended euthanasia in a speech to doctors reported in *The Australian* on 22 June 1995:

> Succeeding generations deserve to be disencumbered of some unproductive burdens . . . [like] the Trobriand Islanders who celebrated impending death with a feast after which the aged went into the bush to die from the effects of poisoned food . . .

The Governor-General would no doubt prefer doctors to use Western pharmaceutical products rather than the poisons found in the Trobriand Islands.

Speaking to *The Canberra Times* about people who are opposed to euthanasia, the politician Don Chipp said:

> I think all these bloody do-gooders and busy-bodies ought to get lost.

Meanwhile it has been alleged, in England, that certain hospital managers have issued instructions telling doctors in intensive care units not to resuscitate heart patients of over 60 more than once. One wonders whether the managers were crafty enough to add that special exceptions should be made for 60-year-old hospital bureaucrats.

On 1 December 1995 a London newspaper reported the following story. A Brighton city councillor and former Mayor was asked to make a charitable donation to a local hospice. She refused to donate and made the following public statement:

> All those old people in hospices ought to be put down . . . I use the term 'put down' advisedly because it is what we say when dealing with animals.

In the real world the interpretation of any current or future laws authorizing euthanasia will not be made by your friendly neighbours, nor yet by my well-meaning little old aunt. Interpretation of the laws will be the responsibility of unelected bureaucrats (such as hospital managers) and of doctors and nurses whose traditional codes of professional ethics are being emasculated, or abolished, by the State. The laws will be drawn up by men and women who speak and think like the former mayor of Brighton, and the Chief Minister of the Northern Territory, and politician Chipp, and Governor-General Hayden.

CHAPTER NINE

Abortion

'Why Abortion?'

David Braine, essay title

This chapter will discuss the idea that induced abortion is an ethically neutral procedure. Theological views will not be examined.

By induced abortion is meant the deliberate destruction of the product of conception while it is still in the womb.

The product of conception has three different names which correspond roughly to three stages in its development. (It should be remembered, though, that the development from conception to birth is a continuous process of growth, not a series of jumps from one state to another.)

The zygote is the cell formed by the union of two gametes. In animals this cell is created by the union of sperm and ovum.

The zygote grows into an embryo.

Eight weeks after conception the human embryo takes a more or less human form and is thereafter called a foetus.

Having explained these terms I shall nevertheless follow what has become a convention in philosophy and refer to the product of conception, in all its stages, as the foetus.

Pro-life and Pro-choice

In the USA and elsewhere anti-abortion groups have given themselves the label pro-life while those who favour legalization

93

of abortion on demand describe themselves as pro-choice. Some 'middle-ground' pro-lifers hold that abortion is virtually always a bad thing but would nevertheless be willing to allow it occasionally in certain special circumstances.

The expression *therapeutic abortion* is not much used these days and when it is used it turns out to be rather elastic. It is taken to include abortion to save the mother's life, abortion to protect her physical health, and abortion for the sake of her psychological health. The term *psychological ill-health* is itself elastic. In practice psychology is used not only to justify abortion for women threatened by identifiable mental illnesses but also for girls and women who have been the victims of incest or rape, women who are poor and isolated, and women students who have not completed their studies. But it seems best to use the expression *therapeutic abortion* in a non-elastic way to mean abortion to save the mother's life. In first-world countries, in modern times, occasions in which abortion is needed to save a mother's life are very rare.

Pro-life groups in general hold that a human foetus is an innocent human being. Some hold that innocent human beings must never be killed in any circumstances; middle-group pro-lifers would allow such killing in certain cases.

Pro-choice groups tend to believe either that a foetus is not a human being, or that (if it is a human being) it lacks rights and interests and cannot sensibly be described as either innocent or guilty.

Pro-life groups hold that a woman's right to procreative freedom is not absolute. It might be that abortion in certain circumstances is the lesser of two evils but no evil, lesser or not, is morally neutral.

Pro-choice groups, even those who say that human reproduction is 'a very serious matter', generally hold that a woman's right to procreative freedom is absolute and should not be impeded.

The best-known pro-life groups, those with the highest profiles, are certain Christian fundamentalist groups in the USA, and the Roman Catholic church, and the clerics of Islam. But such are not the only people hostile to abortion. Traditional Jewish thought is opposed to abortion. So too are many followers of Gandhi, and a number of humanistic atheists and agnostics.

Abortion in the West

In Western countries public opinion and the law have been influenced to some extent by philosophy teachers who deny that human life has intrinsic value or who assert that abortion is an ethically neutral procedure.

Many Western feminists also argue that abortion is ethically neutral. Others believe that the decision to abort is not exactly neutral but is nevertheless a choice which concerns only the pregnant woman. These feminists, like other pro-choice groups, usually say that attempts to influence a woman's decision – for example, by showing pictures of human foetuses – should not be allowed. It is sometimes added that counselling of any kind is an impediment to a pregnant woman's moral freedom. Such restrictions on information and counselling would make abortion unusual among questions of ethics since many other moral matters, even those thought of as personal (for instance divorce), are subject to counselling and open to general discussion.

In Britain the views of officials seem pretty favourable to abortion. Pro-life protesters taking part in non-violent demonstrations are treated unsympathetically by the police and the courts and some magistrates and police officers speak to, and about, pro-life demonstrators rather in the way their forerunners spoke to, and about, conscientious objectors during the First World War. I am informed by a reliable witness that on one occasion pro-life protesters were taunted by police officers who shouted 'It's a pity YOU weren't aborted!'

In France pro-life protesters used to be treated rather more kindly than in Britain but recently French opinion, including government opinion, has hardened against them.

Germany is an interesting case. In East Germany, as in other communist countries, abortion was available on demand up to the sixteenth week; in West Germany, on the other hand, women wanting abortions had first to discuss the matter with professional advisors whose duty it was to look to the protection of the unborn child. Having been advised, women were then free to choose to abort or not. When the two parts of Germany reunited there was much discussion about how to reconcile their disparate laws. At present (1996) the West German law seems to be prevailing. It is not known (to me) whether the advisory arrangements affect the incidence of abortion in Germany.

In the West abortion is not perceived as a method of birth control so much as a kind of fall-back if contraception fails. Nor is it usually defended as a means of curbing population growth though it is now common enough, probably, to be having a significant effect on the birthrate. In the USA, for example, in the late 1980s, there were 400 abortions for every 1,000 live births. Still, Americans who favour the legalization of abortion are not specially worried about population growth as such. In so far as Americans see population control as a good idea they think of it as mainly relevant to people living on Welfare.

Voluntary, Compulsory and Semi-compulsory Abortion

Let's look now at the various social and political contexts in which abortion becomes common.

In some countries abortion is seen as a way of coping with social ills such as unstable marriages, illegitimacy and other forms of single parenthood, welfarism, male violence (rape and incest), and the threat of over-population. When nations neglect these social ills they develop an increasing dependence on abortion as a quick, all-purpose solution. Abortion then becomes more common – but poverty and incest and single parenthood do not go away.

Abortion

The Soviet Union was the first country to legalize abortion in modern times and abortion is still common in communist and ex-communist countries. Soviet law allowed abortion up to the sixteenth week for any woman who requested it. The early Bolsheviks described abortion as a woman's right. This view is still accepted in modern Russia and not only by communists and former communists; for example, it is accepted by the right-wing politician Vladimir Zhirinovsky, who was questioned about the matter on American TV in 1994.

The pro-abortion stance of the USSR had nothing to do with population policies because the rulers of the USSR were in favour of increasing the population rather than reducing it. Under Stalin women were awarded medals for having many children but medals could not serve as much of an encouragement when other factors militated strongly against large families. It seems, too, that abortion was more common in Russia itself than in the Muslim republics in the south and east, indicating that religious beliefs are more important than medals. In the cities severe housing shortages plus the rule forbidding people to own houses, or to rent accommodation from anyone except the State, or to move from one home to another without official permission, meant that ordinary families often did not have room even for one child. According to a news report from Moscow printed in a British newspaper shortly after the breakdown of the Soviet Union the average married woman in Russia could expect to have one or two children and 10–12 abortions during her fertile life. In the same report it was stated that abortion in the USSR was normally carried out without anaesthetics.

In present-day communist China abortion is not only legal but very often compulsory. No urban family in China is supposed to have more than one child and no rural family may have more than two. So if a woman with one or two living children becomes pregnant a second or third time she will be made to undergo abortion willy-nilly. It seems likely that in China, as in Russia, many abortions, especially those occurring under compulsion, would be carried out without anaesthetics.

97

Chinese families used traditionally to limit family size by means of female infanticide. Unwanted baby girls were placed on 'baby towers' where they died of cold and starvation. This traditional practice was condemned by the communist government – or at any rate by its propaganda. In the 1980s in the Chinese city of Chengdu I saw a large billboard with a picture of little girls in school uniform and the message 'A girl is as good as a boy.' But female infanticide has not been abolished by official propaganda and observers report that it is on the increase. Some Sinologists attribute the increase to the government's restrictions on child-bearing. Familes in the countryside can sometimes get away with having more than the two children permitted them but city dwellers face the full rigours of the law. Corruption allows officials and wealthy people to keep on 'trying for a boy' without necessarily resorting to infanticide but even they do not want too many daughters. (The reasons behind the world-wide preference for male children lie beyond the scope of this book.)

In some places abortion is either the only, or the most easily available, method of birth control. Capitalist Japan, like communist China, encourages abortion as its chief method of limiting the growth of population. Unfortunately for Japanese women the medical profession in that country has decreed that the contraceptive pill is unsafe. Because the pill is legally banned, and also no doubt for reasons having to do with male tastes and wishes, abortion and female sterilization are the main methods of birth control. Women in Japan, like women in China and Russia, can expect to undergo many abortions during their fertile lives.

Pro-choice Arguments: Interests, Harms and Rights

In the USA and the UK the commonest view among the best-known teachers of moral philosophy is that it is all right to destroy foetuses. In other words most English-language philosophical writing on the topic of abortion supports the pro-choice position. When philosophy teachers who lecture on practical ethics support the pro-choice view they do so either because they believe human life as such is not special or because they think the human foetus has no rights or interests of its own.

The American professor, Joel Feinberg, was one of the first to write in support of the pro-choice position: his book *The Problem of Abortion* was publioshed in 1973. A few years later Michael Tooley published *A Defense of Abortion and Infanticide*. (Generally speaking philosophy teachers who support abortion also support infanticide.) In *Life's Dominion: An Argument about Abortion, Euthanasia and Individual Freedom* (1993) Ronald Dworkin claims that both the following propositions are true: first, human life, including the life of the embryo, is sacred; second, every woman has an absolute right to abortion on demand. Dworkin must have failed to notice that these two propositions appear to contradict one another. He also claims that the American Bill of Rights guarantees a right to abortion in spite of the fact that the Bill does not mention the matter at all. It was on account of these features, perhaps, that *Life's Dominion* was described by one commentator as 'miraculous'.

Let us look at some of the details of the pro-choice arguments, beginning with those presented by Joel Feinberg. Feinberg claims that a foetus cannot be harmed. He defines harm as the thwarting of interests and states that a foetus has no interests to thwart. But we need to question this proposition; surely even a foetus has an interest in avoiding pain and an interest in not being killed? Suppose we reason that it has no interest in avoiding pain because it cannot feel pain; well, that reasoning might well be wrong. For some scientists now believe that the foetus can feel pain as soon as the central nervous system has begun to develop. The development of the CNS begins quite early and before most real-world abortions take place. One or two academics writing after Feinberg have acknowledged that the foetus might be able to feel pain and so might have an interest in avoiding pain. They hold, though, that if avoidance of pain is the only interest a foetus can have it would still be all right to destroy it provided a pain-killing drug is administered first. This seems a somewhat bizarre conclusion.

Do the interests of any living creature ever relate solely to the avoidance of pain? In the higher species pain is generally accompanied by emotions such as anger or agitation and this is true even when the animal is newborn. Human mothers know that babies in pain look agitated and angry. If we allow that a creature has an interest in avoiding pain we have to also allow that it is capable of mental states.

There are several human rights and interests unrelated to the avoidance of pain and emotion; for instance there is a human right to free expression and a normal human interest in long life. If all interests related solely to the avoidance of pain (and emotion) there would be nothing wrong in killing anyone, old or young, happy or sad, healthy or sick, provided only that the individuals to be killed had no one to mourn for them and that their deaths were rendered physically and psychologically painless by anaesthetic drugs. But that is absurd.

A foetus cannot make any claims because it cannot speak. Does it have the same kind of interest in its own continued existence that we see in children and adults? Michael Tooley answers this question by saying that only creatures who can desire their own continued existence can have an interest in continuing to exist. But to have such a desire, he adds, requires concepts: the concepts of self, experience, existence, continuing life.

Now, if a foetus has no concepts at all it obviously cannot have a concept of pain. Yet at a certain stage of its development it can *suffer* pain. When it reacts to pain–stimulus does that not indicate a desire to avoid pain? Whatever we think about concepts and who or what can possess them, it is clear that living creatures can suffer pain. Whether or not we decide to attribute the *concept* of pain to animals, or to newborn or unborn infants, is much less important than the fact that they show by their behaviour that they suffer pain and desire to avoid it.

Tooley's two premises, viz., that interests require certain desires, and that those desires require certain concepts, are both false.

If the claim that a foetus has no interests, so that its interests cannot be harmed, were correct, the fact that doctors treat foetuses as patients would be quite inexplicable. If foetuses have no interests and no rights why do doctors try to protect them from natural diseases? Why do doctors try to persuade pregnant women not to smoke tobacco or take drugs? Perhaps it will be replied that doctors protect foetuses because these belong to mothers and mothers are patients. But it is no part of a doctor's duty to protect the *property* of their patients.

Anyway, do rights really depend on having current interests and on having the concept of interests? Isn't that a rather far-fetched idea, typical of the ivory tower? The law does not demand the conditions invented by philosophy professors. In English law, for example, a testator can will an estate to a child *ventre sa mere*, that is, to a child which is still inside its mother. If the executors of the will were philosophy teachers they might perhaps attempt to divert the estate to some other beneficiary, thus perpetrating an actionable violation of a legal right.

The child itself, of course, would have to rely on someone else to bring its case to court but that is true for any child, born or unborn.

Pro-Life Arguments:
Human Life and Human Embryology

Let us now consider the nature of human life as it is understood by embryologists and geneticists. For just as our thoughts about animal rights, or vivisection, or factory farming, can be clarified through discussion of the similarities and differences between chimpanzees and human beings, dogs and sheep, mice and bees, so in a somewhat similar way we might hope to clarify our thoughts about abortion by considering the similarities and differences between human foetuses, human newborns, human children and human adults. We cannot decide whether or not abortion is morally neutral unless we know something about the nature of the human foetus and we cannot know the nature of the foetus if we ignore genetics and embryology. It is pointless to say that rights depend on harms if we do not even know what harms a foetus might suffer.

David Braine remarks:

> I do not say that these arguments [i.e. his arguments about the moral significance of the stages in foetal development] are right, but only that they are at least *of the right sort*, if the question is as to when the individual with human life . . . comes into existence.

What kind of entity is the human foetus? Is it a human being? A human individual? Is it part of something else? Is it sentient?

It is clear that a human foetus is a human foetus and not a horse foetus or a cat foetus or whatever. It has the potentiality to turn into a human child but there is no possibility of its turning into a foal or a kitten.

A human foetus, then, is a human entity of some sort.

Should we think of it as part of something else? Perhaps the most famous early slogan of the pro-choice movement was: Women have the right to decide what to do with their own bodies. This suggests that a foetus is similar to a finger, which is indeed part of a body. However, that can't be right because a finger can never develop into a complete animal whereas a foetus can do that if not stopped. A finger will never be independent, its life and growth will always depend on the life and growth of the body of which it is a part. Secondly, when implantation takes place the genetic instruction to implant comes from the (embryonic) foetus, not from the mother. Even at that early stage the foetus has 'genetic independence'.

It might be objected here that, although the human foetus is a living being, it is so undeveloped that destroying it is quite unlike destroying a child or an adult. Or again, it might be objected that there must be a big difference between destroying an early foetus and a late one. In a famous legal decision (*Roe* v. *Wade*, 1973) the US Supreme Court drew a distinction between abortion in the first 3 months, abortion in the second 3 months, and abortion, or induced miscarriage, in the final 3 months. It was ruled that the lawfulness or otherwise of abortion in America depends on how early or late in pregnancy the operation is undertaken, a decision which draws sharp lines between different stages of foetal development. No legal cut-off points can really mirror the gradual but rapid growth of the human organism in the womb, nevertheless the intuitions even of pro-lifers (or anyway, of some pro-lifers) probably support the idea that killing a very early foetus is not as bad as inducing a late miscarriage and then killing the baby as it emerges from the mother's body.

On the other hand many things have been discovered about foetal development since the ruling in *Roe* v. *Wade*. The effects, on the unborn child, of medication, and the mother's smoking or drugging, and chemical pollution, are being examined, and normal and abnormal foetal development is being traced in more and more detail. It is now known (or so it would appear) that development is both more complicated and more rapid than once was thought to be the case.

Is a human foetus a human individual? Is it an individual in the way that a newborn infant is an individual? A newborn infant is distinctively human genetically, and in its physical organs, limbs, features and behaviour. Although it might be the case (as far as we know) that a newborn does not think much, or make many choices, still, it has the potentiality to do those things. It is clear that a new baby is a single creature which has its own characteristic features and its own individual potentialities as well as the qualities and potentialities characteristic of the human species. In other words it is human, it is a being, and it is an individual.

The foetus too has human genetic characteristics, human potentialities, and some distinctive features of its own – for

103

example, it will be male or female, large or small, fair or dark, healthy or unhealthy, and so on.

There is no reason known to biology to deny that there is a human organism present from the moment of conception, and no reason to think that the organism is a part of something else in the way that a finger is a part of something else. But how soon after conception can we speak of this organism as a living individual? When does individual life begin?

In the Middle Ages it was held that the individual life of the foetus begins at quickening, that is, when the mother first feels the child move. Another possible test for individual life is viability, but viability is not a satisfactory notion because it is unclear. Do we mean viability with or without medical assistance? Without medical assistance foetuses have to be 24 to 28 weeks old to survive outside the mother, but medical techniques can reduce that length of time. Modern techniques have occasionally enabled tiny 20-week infants to survive.

Then again it is sometimes argued that until a foetus is viable it is part of its mother's body and from this supposition arises the pro-choice claim that a woman has a right to decide what to do with her own body. But as noted above there is no scientific basis for thinking that the foetus is a part of the woman's body in the way that her fingers are.

Is there a human individual present from the moment of conception? What facts about embryology should be considered here? One such fact, often referred to, relates to twinning. At the very beginning the product of conception is, in a sense, neither one individual nor two; it is unstable as to number, as it were. It might split into two identical twins (or three triplets . . .) or it might remain as one. It used to be thought that twinning remained a possibility up until 14 days after conception, but recent research suggests that the event which eventually produces identical siblings occurs at 5 days. Nevertheless it can be argued that abortion before 14 days, or before 5 days, as the case may be, e.g., by the use of a 'morning after' contraceptive pill, is not really killing because in order to kill a living creature (or creatures) you have to destroy distinct individuals.

As we have already noticed, widespread acceptance of abortion is in part the result of government or community pressures directed against situations perceived as social ills. Misinformation about the nature of the foetus is one of those pressures. According to a recent American TV programme relayed in Britain it appears to be the case that people working in abortion clinics commonly tell pregnant women that the foetus is only a small mass of undifferentiated tissue. That is not true. The foetus has its own genetic code marking it off from other members of the human species and also (of course) from members of other species. Its principal organs begin to develop at 16 days. The central nervous system appears in the 7th week, though it is not agreed, or perhaps not known, whether the anatomical presence of the CNS necessarily means that the system is functioning. In other words, the existence of the early CNS might or might not be associated with the capacity to feel pain. Spontaneous movement becomes possible shortly after 8 weeks and some physiologists believe that capacity to feel pain arrives at the same time, for they interpret certain movements as reactions to pain. At 8 weeks the foetus has a recognizable human shape and is possessed of its main organs, including the brain. At 18 weeks the foetus begins to suck its thumb – a very human activity.

Abortion is a common surgical procedure in the UK, in many States of the USA, and in Japan, China and Russia. It is legal, of course, in all those places. However, because of hospital waiting lists and other factors most abortions take place long after 14 days. Abortion is permitted by law up to the 24th week in Britain and in some circumstances right up to birth. It has to be acknowledged, therefore, that abortion in the real world usually involves destroying a human organism which has already become either one individual or two or three (twins, triplets) and which has already achieved an important degree of organic differentiation. In the case of abortion at or after 20 weeks the organism is viable (with or without the help of modern life-support techniques) and can feel pain.

It follows that a defence of abortion as it happens in the real world would need to show that it is not wrong to destroy pre-natal sentient human individuals. As a result philosophy teachers often argue that, because in their view destroying pre-natal human individuals is not wrong, it cannot be wrong to destroy young infants already born. How young is another question. Sometimes philosophy teachers say that one-month-old infants can be killed, at other times the same people will claim that the upper limit is determined by the infant's acquisition of knowledge of the concept of a person. But explicit knowledge of the concept of a person is something that has to be taught and learnt: it certainly could not be acquired by children under the age of about 2, perhaps not until, 4, or 5, or 7. Do these professors really mean to refer to implicit knowledge? If so shouldn't we ask whether newborn children too might have implicit knowledge for all we know?

Abortion Compared to War

Most people have now come to believe that war is an evil to be avoided whenever possible. Defenders of a Just War theory, defenders of defensive war, even defenders of aggressive war as an adjunct to foreign policy, do not usually say that war is good, or that there would be nothing wrong about allowing it to become a permanent state of affairs. The general view is that war is bad but in some circumstances perhaps inevitable. Statesmen should do whatever can reasonably be done to reduce its likelihood.

Christian pro-lifers, especially Catholics, tend to take a view which in a way parallels that of the total pacifist. For a total pacifist war is always wrong whatever the circumstances. For the total pro-lifer all abortion is always wrong whatever the circumstances. A total pro-lifer will be opposed even to those (now rare) terminations which are carried out solely in order to save the mother's life.

In many Western countries abortion is accepted today as an ordinary medical procedure. Unlike war it is not regarded as an evil to be avoided wherever possible. But in the less-developed nations there has been something of a backlash against attempts to encourage the use of abortion. Religious and other leaders in Africa are saying that Western attempts to persuade poorer nations to legalize abortion are motivated by a fear that population growth among impoverished peoples could force the wealthy West to share its riches.

CHAPTER TEN

Professional Ethics

'Traditions are needed to form a link between institutions and the intentions and valuations of individual men . . . nothing is more dangerous than the destruction of this traditional framework.'

Karl Popper, *Conjectures and Refutations*

The conception of a vocation, or a calling, seems to have come to us from medieval Christianity. In those days certain people were said to be called to a religious life while others had a vocation to follow this or that secular trade, usually the trade practised by their forebears. Yet the idea that particular kinds of work have special obligations must be much older than Christianity for it can be seen in the dialogues of Plato. In *The Republic*, for example, it is said that shepherds are supposed to care for their sheep and doctors for their patients. Socrates, of course, was not happy with the idea that one might be able to extract a satisfactory account of virtue from these or any other special cases. Still, the evidence is that the concept of virtues which pertain to particular kinds of work must have been familiar to him.

After the industrial revolution of the early nineteenth century new economic arrangements allowed workers much more freedom to choose or change their employment than had previously been the case, and perhaps that freedom led them to abandon the idea of being called. Moreover, the kinds of work engaged in probably encouraged new attitudes, because the depersonalized employment found in factories can easily be regarded as nothing more than a rather unpleasant source of income. Nowadays the idea of a vocational ethos belongs only to the liberal professions.

The liberal professions differ from other jobs in that they require a lot of study followed by sophisticated apprenticeships – and there are other differences too, as will be seen below.

The Hippocratic Oath

Medicine provides the best and oldest example of a professional code. It has a long history which begins with the oath of Hippocrates (460–377 BC). Some parts of the Hippocratic Oath are designed to discourage competitive attitudes because competitive attitudes are damaging to doctors and patients alike. The most important aspect, though, has to do with the way in which the code imposes special obligations on the members of the medical profession. There is an obligation to transmit medical knowledge to suitable students who must themselves take the oath. There is an obligation to do what is medically possible to cure the patient and to refrain from harming him or her in any way. There is an obligation to resist sexual and other temptations which may arise during the course of treatment.

Here is an English translation:

> I swear by Apollo the Physician and Asclepius and Hygieia and Panacceia and all the gods and goddesses, making them my witnesses, that I will fulfil according to my best ability and judgement this oath and covenant:
>
> To hold him who has taught me this art as equal to my parents and to live my life in partnership with him, and if he is in need of money to give him a share of mine, and to regard his offspring as equal to my brothers and to teach them this art – if they desire to learn it – without fee; to give a share of precepts and oral instruction and all other learning to my sons and to the sons of him who has instructed me and to pupils who have signed the covenant and have taken an oath according to the medical law, but to no one else.
>
> I will apply dietetic measures for the benefit of the sick accord-

ing to my ability and judgement; I will keep them from harm and injustice.

I will neither give a deadly drug to anybody if asked for it, nor will I make a suggestion to this effect. Similarly I will not give to a woman an abortive remedy. In purity and holiness I will guard my life and my art.

I will not perform surgery, even for the stone, but will leave such procedures to the experts in that field.

Whatever houses I may visit I will come for the benefit of the sick, remaining free of all intentional injustice, of all mischief, and in particular of sexual relations with either male or female patients whether slave or free.

What I may see or hear in the course of the treatment or even outside the treatment in regard to the lives of men, which must not on any account be spread abroad, I will keep to myself, holding that it is shameful to speak of such things.

Ludwig Edelstein reasons that Hippocrates and his students were members of the school founded in the sixth century BC by the philosopher and mathematician Pythagoras. Pythagoreans were opposed to suicide, to abortion and to the slaughter of animals in sacrifices to the gods.

It strikes me that the practices attributed to the Pythagoreans resemble those of modern supporters of 'alternative' medicine. Both say that poor health can be the result of faulty diet or other faulty living; they both believe that pharmacological products should be used, if at all, only when simpler, more natural cures fail; and they do not practise surgery.

Special Obligations

Why do professional people have special obligations? One reason is that if a government discourages special obligations it soon becomes a tyranny. Parental and filial duties were greatly undermined in the Soviet Union and as a result of that the regime was enabled to condemn people to forced labour on the say-so of their own relatives. In communist China during the so-called cultural revolution the special relationship between schools and pupils, and the respect felt by students for their teachers, were savagely condemned. One consequence was that a whole generation of children lost the chance of getting a reasonable education.

The other reasons for having special codes can be most easily demonstrated in the case of medicine.

It is very important that the law of the land be backed up by a code of medical ethics because medical training gives doctors the power of life and death over other people. Untrained men and women cannot easily tell whether or when the expertise is being misused but other doctors can. These facts give rise to a genuine need for professional self-regulation; and it is a need, not a privilege. The professional code does not replace the law of the land but supplements it. The case is otherwise with work like journalism, and broadcasting, and so on. In those areas self-regulation does not supplement any law but is permitted to exist as a substitute for legislation. A good example is the Hays Office, a body set up in Hollywood by the film industry to monitor films for sexual content. In newspapers, television and film, self-regulation is a privilege and as such can be abused.

Special codes are useful for the further reason that some people have duties to do things which in others would count as acts of supererogation. For example, doctors and paramedics have a duty of rescue (unfortunately this duty has been seriously undermined, especially in the USA, by legal arrangements which encourage accident victims to sue their helpers and rescuers).

Thirdly, codes are needed because it is sometimes necessary that professionals be given permission to act in ways that are forbidden to others. Doctors are allowed to cut people open and to see people undressed; lawyers often have to be given permission to handle their clients' money.

Possessing special powers and special permissions means that professional folk are subjected to unusual temptations which they

111

have to be warned against. As we have just seen, the Hippocratic Oath warns doctors against sexual temptation and the temptation to gossip.

Now it might be argued that every group of workers should have special codes of conduct. For example, there could be a code warning chefs against temptations associated with cooking. After all, a chef could be tempted to pretend that the ingredients of a dish are different from what he actually uses; should he be given special ethical rules forbidding this? Well, although a code for chefs might perhaps be useful it is not really necessary because it does not take special chef-like skills to detect the kind of cheating which could be associated with the work of cookery and perpetrated in a kitchen. The misdeeds of doctors, on the other hand, can often only be detected by other medical practitioners. Moreover chefs, unlike doctors, have no special privileges allowing them to do things which would be immoral in others. Untrained persons pretending to be surgeons constitute a serious risk to the lives of people needing operations; but if a non-chef offers to cook you a meal he is not doing anything wrong.

The Other Professions

The exceptional powers and permissions of professional people are the result of their having expertise and difficult knowledge. The temptations associated with special powers and permissions generate a need for special restrictions. It would seem, then, that scientists and university teachers should also adopt ethical codes. For whether or not a scientist or a professor is working well or badly, whether or not he or she is up to no good, is often something that only another expert can detect. In that way the nature of academic and scientific work is somewhat similar to medicine and the law.

I personally think it would be a good thing if scientific associations drew up codes of professional conduct for their members and a good thing if university teachers did the same. But that is most unlikely to happen, especially in the case of scientific research. Experimental science has traditions very different from those of the older professions. There is no special idea of service because scientists rarely work for individuals. If they are not teachers they are usually employed by governments or business companies. They are taught to believe that they themselves have no duty to consider the moral implications of their research: moral decisions, they often say, must be taken either by their employers or by 'society as a whole'.

The British biologist J. B. S. Haldane said:

> I am one of the relatively rare professional scientists who realize vividly, if inadequately, the importance for ethics of the work which we are doing.

Would one be happy to hear a doctor say 'I am one of the relatively *rare* doctors who realize the importance for ethics of the work we are doing'? Are ethical doctors *rare*?

It is true, probably, that doctors don't often consciously think about ethical principles. That is partly because they don't usually have to. They don't have to because they work within a tradition which is imbued with the ideal of service, governed (at least until very recently) by bedrock taboos such as the taboo on killing, and regulated by professional associations which still have some clout. None of this is true of scientists. (However, academic scientists, like other teachers, do have some idea of service because their 'clients' are individuals, i.e., students.)

Do academics have special powers and privileges? The question is not easy to answer because academies differ a great deal and so do academic duties. The work of university teaching, and the conditions of employment, are more diverse than is the case in medicine. In many countries academics are civil servants. People working in traditional universities generally engage in both teaching and research but recently in Britain there have been government moves to classify institutions into two types, those that teach and those that undertake research.

The task of doctors, of course, is to promote the health of their patients. Lawyers promote justice (or ought to). What do universities do?

The two traditional tasks of universities are the advancement of knowledge and the communication of knowledge. Some would add a third, namely, the training of students for the world of work; however, the second task can be regarded as in some sense incorporating the third.

In the West the rights claimed by scholars and scientists include freedom of speech, and even in societies where such freedom is generally forbidden academics are given, or might claim, the right to at least discuss their work with one another, or to publish their research; and so on. In societies which allow the ordinary citizen freedom of speech academics are given, or else might demand, that they suffer no special restrictions in this regard.

Academics also claim a right to choose what to teach and how to teach it; the right to choose their (junior) colleagues; the right (and the duty) to set examinations or to grade students; and the freedom to choose one's area of research. But academics in China and Korea do not have these rights. Moreover it is an unfortunate fact that pressures from the so-called managerial culture currently reigning in the West tend to reduce academic freedom.

Rights and freedom entail responsibility. An academic ethics would codify responsibilities in the areas of research and teaching respectively and would also warn against possible temptations.

Temptations in Research, Administration, Teaching

There are many temptations in the area of research. It is tempting to take sole credit for the work of a team (if one can). It is tempting to fake results for the sake of money, or fame, or a

114

better job. It is tempting to plagiarize the work of lesser-known people (for example, by copying work published in reputable but obscure journals). It is tempting for editors of learned journals to ignore papers and research results identified with junior people, or with people judged to be unimportant, and to kowtow to people thought to be powerful.

Here is a story which exemplifies a state of affairs which is not utterly unknown. The editor of an international journal receives a paper from a junior academic called Mortimer Jones and mistakenly thinks it comes from a famous scholar called Cledwyn Jones; he writes back:

> Dear Cledwyn,
>
> I am delighted to accept your paper which will be published in our next issue.

Just in time he realizes that the youthful Mortimer is not the famous Cledwyn, so rewrites his letter as follows:

> Dear Mr Jones,
>
> I am sorry to say I have decided not to publish your paper.

There can be a temptation to propagandize, that is, to teach controversial material in ways that discourage critical examination. Propaganda includes distortion, and a refusal to look at certain theories and opinions, and a refusal to recommend books which are opposed to one's own views. It can involve ridiculing dissidents and concealing facts.

In teaching there is surely a duty not to neglect one's students. One ought not to ignore particular pupils or certain classes of pupils, for example the weaker ones or the females, or write dishonest references for favourite (or unfavourite) students, or grade exam scripts and dissertations in unfair ways.

Temptations can arise in administration. Apart from general laziness the tempting deeds include overrating one's own students, writing harsh references because of an egotistical desire to appear as a person of very high standards, supporting job candidates who share one's beliefs, refusing to appoint a rival, and blackmailing colleagues by saying 'If you appoint professor so-and-so to a post here I will simply refuse to work with him.'

Academics are also subject to sexual temptations. Young people are often sexually attractive, so that temptation can be part of academic life, as it were, just as it is sometimes part of a doctor's life.

In January 1995 British newspapers carried a report about a 44-year-old married lecturer who was sacked after a complaint from one of his students. He had sent her this letter:

> Submit! I want you to bring your body to my room wrapped in an elegant dress, or send a note saying 'I give in'.

At a tribunal set up to consider the matter the accused man alleged unfair dismissal, stating 'I am no lecher' and claiming that sexual liaisons between teachers and students were 'the norm'. (I have not been able to trace any reports about the tribunal's final decision.)

The rule *no sex with students* used to be honoured in universities once upon a time and perhaps still is in some of the older and more traditional places. It seems, though, that nowadays the rule is not by any means universally observed. It there any point in discussing a taboo which has disappeared? Is it not a case of shutting the stable door after the horse has bolted? Well, it could be interesting to consider whether the need for the taboo was genuine or imaginary and whether the need remains even if the taboo itself has gone. It would be interesting, too, to find out whether there is a case for introducing new and different restrictions. Times change. If the taboos of yesterday seem indefensible today they could come to be regarded, tomorrow, as essential, though perhaps for different reasons (or for the old reasons under new names). For example, rules against sexual harassment have somewhat the same effect as a ban on sexual liaisons.

The rule *no sex with students* was thought by many to exist for the protection of students. Some have argued that teachers are looked up to rather as parents are. It is claimed that sexual encounters with parent figures have a psychological effect similar to that of incest or child abuse. However, I don't think many professors are perceived as symbolic parents. After all, they themselves can be childish. The lecturer referred to above was unloading his own puerile fantasies onto the student rather than the other way around.

If students do look up to their teachers that is partly because young people tend to be idealistic and trusting, and it is wrong, of course, to take advantage of anyone's trust and idealism. On the other hand it is said that students nowadays are so sexually sophisticated that the exploitation, if any, is mutual. Still, mutual exploitation does not appear on the face of it to be much better than the one-way version.

If there is no rule against university lecturers having sex with students ought there to be a rule against school teachers doing the same thing with their students? Readers might like to consider for themselves how best to answer this question.

The rule against sex with students protected the academy itself from corruption. Bribes can take the form of sexual favours and professors are not necessarily immune to bribery. Mutual sexual exploitation can damage the academy, as happened in the following case (names have been changed): Dr Boff, a lecturer in a British educational institution, was appointed to the post of Head of Department in a College of Design in another country. A former student, allegedly Boff's lover, applied for a lecturership in the College, falsely claiming to have an Honours Diploma from the British establishment. Dr Boff gave the job to his alleged lover, knowing that the young man had in fact not completed the Diploma course and would not have been awarded honours in any case. The College of Design was thus lumbered with an unqualified lecturer who was protected by a powerful member of the Faculty.

The Special Case of Philosophy

What ways, if any, of violating academic ethics occur in philosophy?

Philosophy consists largely in analysis, speculation and the construction of theories. It can happen that those who teach the subject come to embrace improbable theories just for the fun of it. That in turn can produce a kind of unseriousness, a kind of insincerity. One or two famous French philosophy professors (who must remain nameless) display a very irritating combination of boastfulness and frivolity.

To be serious is not the same thing as being solemn and humourless. In my opinion it is possible to be both serious and witty at the same time, and Wittgenstein goes further: he said he could easily imagine a serious work of philosophy which was made up entirely of jokes.

The temptation to do what leads to reputation and fame is always present to the academic. It is possible for a philosophy professor to make a name by inventing a ludicrous and counter-intuitive thesis. It is possible to become well-known outside academic circles by visiting hospitals and giving 'expert' advice (the more astounding the better) on ethical problems.

Philosophy teachers should try to remember that speculations which have no bad effects in the lecture room might easily have appalling results in the real world. It is self-evident that Applied Ethics is particularly risky because its whole point is to apply philosophy to the world.

A professional code arising from the powers, permissions and temptations specific to the academic life ought to include the duty to set out evidence fully and fairly; and the duty to acknowledge all one's sources; and a general willingness to accept criticism. There should be a recognized obligation to think about the probable real-world consequences of one's teaching and research. Academics should ask themselves from time to time whether their enquiries might have bad results. It would be good if researchers adopted a code forbidding them to acquire knowledge by painful or dangerous or secret experiments on human beings. It would be good if researchers refused to undertake trivial research for the sake of money. It would be good if they were not asked to undertake work involving secrecy – partly because universities are committed to the extension of knowledge and also because secret things might turn out to be dangerous to the community.

Business and the Professions

The rights and freedoms of academics are currently being challenged by advocates of 'accountability'. What lies behind this challenge is the thought that universities ought not to be allowed to teach and study whatever they like because students and professors are often funded by the taxpayer. Universities should promote knowledge in areas judged to be useful by the taxpayers themselves. (In reality judgements as to what is useful and what is not are made by bureaucrats.)

There is a widespread belief in British political circles that academics and doctors ought to behave like business people; they *ought* to be motivated by monetary considerations, even if they are not. Doctors too should be prepared to engage in, or fall in with, the 'businesslike' practices enjoined upon them by government.

Business is in a sense a fragmented activity in which it is taken for granted that there will be clashes between the interests of management, stockholders and workers. In medicine as traditionally conceived the interests of patient and doctor, or general practitioner and specialist, are not thought of as being in conflict; similarly, professors don't really think that students are 'the enemy' (though they sometimes pretend to). In other words, business enterprises maximize competition between practitioners in the same field whereas the professions minimize it. Professional people, unlike business people, are supposed to cooperate with one another and they often work in teams (in clinics for example). To laypeople, unfortunately, professional cooperation can appear as a kind of elitism.

Britain has recently seen many political attempts to force doctors and scholars and scientists to mimic the behaviour of business managers. These pressures are probably quite destructive. They tend to reduce the influence of generally accepted codes of ethics and this in turn will eventually lead to the disappearance of the moral thinking underlying the codes.

PART FOUR

Ideology and Value

CHAPTER ELEVEN

Feminism and Masculism

'Only a male intellect clouded by the sexual drive could call the stunted, narrow-shouldered, broad-hipped and short-legged sex the fair sex . . . It lies in the nature of women to regard everything simply as a means of capturing a man, and their interest in anything else is only simulated, is only a detour, i.e., amounts to coquetry and mimicry. Women are thorough and incurable philistines . . . they are the inferior sex in every respect.'

Arthur Schopenhauer, *Essay on Women*

'Male Chauvinist Pigs!'

Feminist war-cry (late twentieth century)

Feminism is a word which makes right-wing journalists reach for their guns. But if feminism as such is a bad thing mustn't masculism also be bad? Conversely if there is nothing wrong with masculism as such can there be anything wrong with feminism? If brotherhood is good how can sisterhood be bad?

The answers depend, of course, on what is meant by *masculism* and *feminism*. Each is a weasel word which refers to a range of possible attitudes and beliefs and a corresponding range of actions and activities. Hence there can be no simple definition of either term, only a list of the various kinds of belief and action which it refers to. In other words there are different species of feminism and masculism; some are morally neutral, others morally significant, and others again are irrational or even mad.

A study of the history of ideas indicates that masculism in the past has too often consisted of crackpot speculations about the nature of Woman capital W. Unfortunately feminists, especially

123

contemporary feminists, also engage in crackpot speculation from time to time.

Masculist and feminist behaviour, beliefs and attitudes range from the benign to the malignant, from the reasonable to the irrational. Traditional masculism comprises a number of assumptions about the nature of men and the nature of women and about the social roles proper to each. The activities stemming from those beliefs include pleasant deeds of chivalrous solicitude and protectiveness and malignant actions like coarse jokes and wife-beating and unjust laws. Masculist attitudes to women range from kindly condescension to real contempt.

Feminism is a reaction to masculism. Since women have not usually had much say in law-making the activities associated with feminism have until recently been confined to authorship and propaganda and protest behaviour. Typical feminist attitudes to men range ambivalently from fear and dislike to affectionate tolerance.

The Philosophy and Science of Sex

Philosophy and science of sex have to do with a real or imagined natural or spiritual necessity underlying the different social roles and social status allotted to men and women respectively. The differences in roles and status are explained, or explained away, as the case may be, by theories about the mind and the soul or by quasi-scientific speculations in biology and psychology. Until the second half of the twentieth century the philosophy and science of sex tended to support traditional masculist attitudes. Thinkers typically assumed without question that the conventional notions about what is natural and unnatural, normal or abnormal, male and female behaviour are in general correct. Even when scientific theories about human nature changed as science and philosophy changed, the social messages remained pretty similar. One big message was that women are less able than men in all but one or two fields. Women are good at nurturing children and old people and sick people and they are adept at running a home and at supporting and soothing their menfolk. Men are good at everything else: philosophy, art, science, politics and so on. Another message appears in the philosopher Rousseau's book *Émile and Sophie*. Rousseau's view is that little girls exist in order to serve the interests of little boys and grown women exist in order to serve the interests of men.

Feminists are often accused of exaggeration and hysteria and similar sins and crimes. But if one reads the works of philosophical masculists one sees that exaggeration and hysteria are not a female prerogative. The history of male thinking about the nature of women reveals some weird brainstorms.

Aristotle, for example, held the opinion that menstrual blood is a fluid which has failed to turn into semen. This idea served as support for his theory that women are people who have failed, as it were, to turn into men. However, Aristotle was writing at the very dawn of biological science and for that reason he cannot really be blamed for holding strange views.

Over two thousand years later, in 1927, the distinguished biologist, Julian Huxley (1887–1975), wrote as follows:

Is there a difference between Man and Woman as finished products, and if so how great is this difference? . . . granted the difference, how much of it is due to inborn differences between the sexes, how much to the different social and domestic functions of the two sexes, how much to the influence of tradition and education?

(Isn't it rather odd that he uses the capital letters M and W? The word Man with a capital letter usually refers to the species, yet Huxley the biologist cannot possibly have thought that Woman capital W is a separate species from Man.)

Huxley began to answer his question by stating that science proves the existence of many important inborn differences between the sexes. He went on to imply that biological differences are sufficient to justify the usual conservative social practices.

125

Scientist Huxley, however, was a very mild kind of masculist. More malign forms of the ism can be seen in the writings of certain philosophers, notably Arthur Schopenhauer and Otto Weininger. With a few exceptions (Plato, Condorcet, J. S. Mill) male philosophers seem to be even more prone than the man in the street to harbour weird ideas about women.

Arthur Schopenhauer's misogyny is quite extreme and so too is that of his follower Otto Weininger. Weininger's works were admired by Wittgenstein, who recommended them to the Cambridge philosopher G. E. Moore. Moore apparently found Weininger's work pretty unappealing.

Folk Theories and Folklore

The low status of women in folk theory is manifested in parental reactions to the arrival of boy babies and girl babies. In traditional societies (in China for instance, and among the Inuit people, and in old-fashioned Islamic communities) the birth of a boy is welcomed with joy while the birth of a girl is a fairly serious disappointment.

The status difference between men and women can be embodied in law (as was formerly the case in the West) or simply in tribal custom. When travelling in Fiji I was told about a present-day custom relating to motor vehicles. It seems that in Fiji women are not allowed to sit in the front seat of a motor car because the front seat has high status. If the vehicle is a lorry or a truck the women have to stand up, or sit on the floor, in the back section, along with whatever goods the truck is carrying.

Here is another example: in rural Pakistan I once saw a crowd of children surrounding a group of tourists and begging for chocolate and pens. Most of the children were little boys but a few little girls tried to join in. The boys kept driving the girls away, and as they did so their faces took on expressions of righteous indignation at the presumption of the females. It was apparent from their behaviour and from their faces that in the boys' opinion begging is man's work.

Philosophy and science and folk theories and law are not the only ways in which the different roles and statuses allotted to men and women are expressed. Politicians and journalists, dramatists and novelists, have all defended the differences from time to time. The teachings of religion often contain injunctions about the correct way for women to behave and the correct way for men to treat women. In the Koran, for example, there are several passages which instruct men in the proper ways to treat wives and concubines and female captives.

The Natural and the Unnatural

Not all differences between human beings are natural, some are social. But unreflective people don't always find it easy to distinguish between what is natural and what is socially created. The Hindu system of caste, for instance, looks like a social creation to non-Hindus but seems to have the force of an ineluctable natural law for the Hindus themselves. Like the Holy Wills imagined by Kant, Hindus follow the moral law – i.e., the caste rules – almost as if these were laws of nature.

Every known society expects men and women to behave differently.

In Western thinking nowadays women, or anyway non-feminist women, are believed to be more soft-hearted than men. They are credited with special intuitive faculties that enable them to understand human psychology and individual personalities. Women are 'good with people'. Men are supposed to be less emotional than women yet at the same time much more in the grip of their sexual drives. They are supposed to be more courageous, better able to deal with danger, and 'good with machines'. They are supposed to have a natural gift for abstract thought and a gift for understanding political and economic issues.

127

Ideology and Value

Anthropologists have reported that human beings tend to invest the natural bodily differences between the sexes with symbolism. All societies impose norms on top of the biological facts. Social norms having to do with sex differ from one place to another and from one era to another, and similarly the symbolism associated with sex also differs. So we might say that each society has its own ways of doing these things.

In some countries women are thought to be too weak to undertake manual work, in others they are regarded as the appropriate bearers of heavy burdens (on their heads).

Some societies feel that art and poetry and music mostly belong to men while dancing mostly belongs to women. In other communities the creation of art and poetry and fiction and music are all seen as sissy pursuits which real men do not engage in. In the nineteenth century the majority of (local) novels published in America and Australia seem to have been written by women. In Australia today it can still happen that actors and male dancers are regarded with suspicion.

Sometimes women are expected to show a love of dress and jewels and decoration, while in other times and places it is the men who adorn themselves. At the beginning of the nineteenth century in England and Europe men and women alike wore silks and lace and bright colours, but towards the end of the century, when ladies were wearing the beautiful dresses depicted in the paintings of the French Impressionists, the gentlemen clothed themselves in undecorated suits of sombre hue, often black. Yet military dress uniforms have always been extremely elegant, and in the old universities of Oxford and Cambridge the recipients of honorary degrees (still mainly males) wear elaborate ceremonial academic bonnets and gowns, the bonnets made of black velvet and the gowns of gorgeously coloured silks.

In spite of variation in detail the underlying implications of symbols and norms seem to be much the same everywhere. Roughly speaking, male is good, strong, fully conscious, clever, while female is less good, less conscious, less strong and not so clever. Symbolic connections are made between the male–female

128

dichotomy and the good–bad, brighter–darker, higher–lower dichotomies of sun and moon, mind and matter, sky and earth, day and night.

There is something of a parallel here with racial attitudes. In countries where light-skinned people and dark-skinned people live side by side it is the dark-skinned who always have the lower status. There is no rationality about this, it is merely a fact reflecting what looks like an almost universal species of unreason buried deep in the human brain.

Sex and Gender

It is fashionable at present to use the word *gender* in place of the word *sex*. One reason is that in current usage the word sex has come to refer, not to the biological differences between males and females, but to sexual intercourse. The word *gender* has a wider use and therefore seems more genteel since sexual intercourse is not always regarded as a polite topic of conversation. *Gender*, however, is not a good label for a biological difference. Since we need a distinction between the biological and social let us use the word *sex* to refer to biological difference and the word *gender* in connection with social roles.

The sex difference is natural, it is not created by society, and its importance relates to reproduction, sexual love and sexual attraction. Gender is a grammatical term which has been taken over by feminists and others to describe certain social structures. In its ordinary sense it refers to the classification of nouns and pronouns into masculine and feminine (and neuter). English has a three-way classification and applies it in a realistic way – for in English only living creatures are 'he' or 'she' while inanimate objects are 'it'. In the French language, by contrast, every noun is either of masculine or of feminine gender. Thus in French even inanimate objects are all either 'he' or 'she'.

The extension of the meaning of the word gender from

grammar to social structures is surely very apt. Grammatical gender is an artificial analogue of natural sex, a kind of imaginary sexuality which in many languages is attributed to chairs and tables as well as to animals. It is an artificial structure which mimics, as it were, the natural biological difference. The new or feminist sense of the word *gender* rests on a similar analogy. *Gender* in this new sense refers to artificial structures made up of social distinctions, which mimic, as it were, the natural biological difference.

To insist that the new usage is incorrect is foolishly pedantic because new word-usages appear all the time. If new meanings are perspicuous and useful there is no reason to reject them and often good reason to accept them.

What do Feminists Want?

As noted above, feminism is a reaction to masculism. Feminists everywhere have always concentrated much energy on describing, and condemning, the injustices suffered by women as the result of laws made by men. They point out that for most of history women have had little or no political power. In the West until this century laws for women were always made by men and elsewhere in the world this is still largely the case. The rules made by one sex to be obeyed by the other are sometimes manifestly irrational. For instance, men have made arrangements whereby women could not attend universities, giving as one of the reasons the supposed fact that women do not have enough intellectual power to be able to study abstract concepts (such as the concepts of mathematics) or technical skills (such as the skills needed by physicians and surgeons). But making rules to prevent what is not possible must surely be a redundant activity. It is as if someone made a law to prevent men from getting pregnant. Bans exist to prevent people from doing what they can or might do, not what they can't do. There is no need to prevent people from doing what cannot be done, by them, in the first place. The existence of rules to keep women out of universities, or to restrict the numbers enrolling, is enough to show that the rule-makers secretly believed that women might be capable of academic study.

Feminists also challenge customs. They believe that customary social distinctions often work against women's interests and women's freedom. Traditional notions help guarantee that political and other power remains in the hands of men.

Even the conventions of dress have been challenged. There have been campaigns against clothing which is dangerous to health (tight stays), against uncomfortable fashions (high collars, scratchy wool), dress that takes a lot of time to get into and out of (too many buttons), and dress which hampers movement, for example spiked heels and crinoline skirts, both of which make it impossible to run. For a long time conventional dress made it difficult for ladylike women to engage in any form of physical exercise. (Some experts even said that women, or perhaps just ladies, could be damaged by physical exertion.) Amelia Bloomer (1818–94), an American feminist, campaigned for 'rational dress', advocating a trouser-like garment, named after her, which could be worn by lady cyclists. The idea of women wearing trousers, however baggy and concealing, produced outrage in some and ribald amusement in others. Reference to bloomers is still regarded as somewhat comical even by people who know nothing of the rough jokes made about Mrs B. in her own day.

Four Kinds of Feminism

Feminism comes in waves and takes different forms, some of which are rational and others less so. (Perhaps the same is true of anti-racism.)

It seems pretty obvious that humanity is a two-sex species. Yet, strange to say, people, both male and female, have written

131

as if there is really only one sex, the male. Great thinkers have formed hypotheses according to which a woman is a kind of defective man. Schopenhauer, for example, seems to think that human females are sick and childish males, while Freud states in so many words that because women do not have male sexual organs they are in some sense castrated.

The idea that there is really only one sex can also be seen in those who adopt a belief-system which we could label the feminism of the androgynous ideal. According to those who espouse the androgynous ideal the best of all possible worlds would be one where the different roles allotted to the two sexes were abolished altogether. Even conception, pregnancy and mothering ought to be abolished. The science of the future, it is argued, will make it possible for conception, 'pregnancy' and 'birth' to take place in test-tubes and laboratories. Men and women might still be required to donate sperm and eggs but the products of these would then be grown in a test-tube or other artificial environment, freeing women from pregnancy and childbirth. In this ideal world of the future the children so created would be reared in institutions, freeing women from the task of mothering.

The androgynous ideal incorporates the view that all traditional feminine roles without exception are the result of social conditioning. I surmise that feminists who hold to the androgynous ideal tend to use the words sex and gender interchangeably while those who reject that ideal do not.

To my mind this particular variety of feminism is crackpot.

Another strand of feminist ideology makes a much less spectacular claim: it merely states that the thinking of women is more likely than male thinking to protect the interests of women.

Is this true? Well, most, though not all, of the people who defend the interests of women have been women, while most, though not all, of the individuals who've attacked those interests, in writing and by voting and so on, have been men.

However, Schopenhauer (amongst others) denies that women ever do support the interests of women:

132

women are by nature enemies ... Even when they pass one another in the street they look at one another like Guelphs and Ghibellines ... when two women exchange compliments it sounds much more ludicrous than when two men do so.

Feminists will reply that senseless enmity between women, and the desire to please and placate the male, are not as common as men suppose. When enmity between women occurs spontaneously it is not a fact of nature but the result of the dependent status decreed by society. Dependency causes women to fear other women and makes them vulnerable to male propaganda. Independence armours them against fear and also to some extent against propaganda.

A third variety of feminism, and one that is important in the academies nowadays, is a theory about methodologies. It claims that women have special ways of using their intellects which differ from the male way. This belief gives rise to the idea that there can be feminist science and feminist epistemology.

Do women have special ways of using their intellectual powers? Can there really be such things as feminist science and feminist philosophy? Susan Haack describes that idea as 'a fashionable kind of intellectual apartheid of the sexes' and 'a reversion to the notion of "thinking like a woman"' which she finds 'disquietingly reminiscent' of traditional sexist (i.e., masculist) stereotypes. Like many 'old' feminists Haack holds the view that the intellect has no sex. Anyone trying to discover truth, anyone wanting to 'figure out how things are' will have to rely on the same things: Haack mentions perception, introspection and theory-construction, to which we might add testimony and experimentation. All these things are available in principle to the female brain as well as to the male. (I say in principle because other, subsidiary, necessities, such as libraries and laboratories, have often been closed to women.)

Haack writes:

Differences in cognitive style, like differences in hand-writing, seem more individual than sex-determined ... It is true, I think,

133

that in the social sciences and biology theories which are not well-supported by the evidence have sometimes come to be accepted by scientists, most often male scientists, who have taken stereotypical ideas of masculine and feminine behavior uncritically for granted . . .

Those who think that criticisms of sexism in scientific theorizing require a new, feminist epistemology insist that we are obliged, in the light of these criticisms, to acknowledge political considerations as legitimate ways to decide between theories. *But on the face of it these criticisms suggest exactly the opposite conclusion – that politics should be kept out of science.* [my italics]

Feminists working in the history and philosophy of science like to dig up evidence which shows that the romantic picture of the scientist as a pure seeker after truth is not accurate. And their digging is by no means unsuccessful. Male scientists, especially biologists and psychologists, have indeed displayed prejudice against women, and have indeed engaged in academic politics from time to time, and in propaganda too. All this tends to make people feel cynical about science as well as about scientists, cynical even about the possibility of ever discovering the truth about anything. The very notion of truth itself is called into question.

Haack remarks that the label 'feminist epistemology' suggests that philosophy and science *ought* to be politicized. This is dangerous for epistemology itself because it presupposes that disinterested inquiry is impossible, that truth is a meaningless word. But there is such a thing as genuine inquiry. Genuine inquiry is best advanced by people who want to find out how things really are, and who are persistent, and not dogmatic. Inquiry which, contrariwise, is dominated by politics, is a sham. The fact that some males conduct what are effectually sham inquiries is no good reason for women to follow suit. If feminists insist on copying the intellectual practices which they condemn in men they reduce philosophy and science and the study of history into batches of oppositional propaganda whose acceptability can only be settled via tests of strength. And who will win those tests? If feminists give up believing in truth and reason they will paint themselves into a corner from which it will not be easy to escape.

Finally, there is a variety of feminism which has to do with emotions and emotional attitudes. It claims that women's attitudes and emotions and ways of forming relationships are radically different from men's. It insists that women are intellectually similar to men but psychologically different overall. Nothing about merit and very little about ideal social roles can be inferred from the similarities and differences; all we can say, according to these feminists, is that women are either just as good as men or even actually better. (In defence of the thesis that women are better than men they claim that women have open minds, men's minds are closed; women are sensitive, men are insensitive; women are constructive, men are destructive; women naturally love peace, men by nature really prefer war and crime; women are intuitive, men have no intuitions worth mentioning; women behave better than men because they are not pig-headed.)

Is it true that women's emotions are different from men's? Are there natural differences between male psychology and female psychology?

It seems to me that in some circumstances women feel more deeply than men do. Quite a few men are protective towards their own small children but the protectiveness of (most) women towards their babies is on a wholly different scale of intensity. Then again I think that women are usually (though not always) more patient with the foibles of small children than men are. Some will say that these facts, if they are facts, are a 'mere' matter of instinct. But so what? Don't men have instincts too? Are all human instincts to be ignored or deplored? Are instincts completely irrelevant to human life and human morality? Surely not.

Extremist feminists wish to deny these facts about the instinctive behaviour patterns of men and women. They seem to think the facts are derogatory to women; to my mind that is far from being the case.

If we look at the emotions in general and not at the special examples of reproduction and nurturing it seems fairly clear that

135

there is enormous variation between individual women, just as there is between individual men.

According to this fourth school of thought feminists should work to make sure that society comes to understand that the intellect has no sex. They should also work to make sure that people recognize the value of certain specifically feminine skills and virtues which until now have been consistently undervalued in all nations. More should be done to persuade people that these feminine skills and virtues ought to be valued just as highly as masculine skills and virtues.

Since feminism (like masculism) is an ambiguous word, the hostility of right-wing journalists to feminism is intellectually careless (at best) and a manifestation, perhaps, of some personal animus (at worst).

CHAPTER TWELVE

Freedom of Thought and Expression

'[The people] have a right, an indispensable, indefeasible, divine
right to that most dreaded and envied kind of knowledge, I mean
of the characters and conduct of their rulers.' (1765)

John Adams (1735–1826)

'If his wife can't trust him why should we?'

Ross Perot, on the private lives of politicians

Most democracies claim to have allowed citizens a right to speak
and write freely on virtually any subject. Sometimes the claim is
partly belied by laws such as Britain's Official Secrets Act, widely
believed to have been used by politicians to hide their own
misdeeds. Nevertheless freedom of speech is taken to be highly
valuable even by those who sometimes try to suppress it for
personal or political reasons.

This right is often proclaimed in written constitutions, the
best-known example being the First Amendment to the American Bill of Rights:

Congress shall make no law respecting the establishment of religion, or prohibiting the free exercise thereof; or abridging the
freedom of speech or of the press or the right of the people to
peacefully assemble, and to petition the government for a redress
of grievances.

Why exactly is freedom of thought and expression regarded as
valuable and worth protecting?

137

Ideology and Value

Power

Should freedom of expression be valued because it makes a nation strong?

During the 1950s freedom of speech in the USA was endangered by the activities of the late Senator Joseph McCarthy who accused many public figures of being secret communists. These men and women were made to appear before the House [of Congress] Un-American Activities Committee, where they were asked about their own political beliefs and those of their friends. Many people, including academics, film writers, playwrights and journalists, lost their jobs during the so-called McCarthy Era, in a few cases because they confessed to having once been supporters of the communist party, more often for refusing to testify at all or for refusing to testify against their friends. Some were gaoled for perjury or contempt of Congress. McCarthy's power ended rather abruptly when he accused some high-up army officers of being secret communists. And by deciding to appear on television he unwittingly caused ordinary viewers to distrust him.

The relevance of these facts is that some people said that McCarthy's attack on freedom of speech and opinion was one of the reasons why America dropped behind the USSR in the Space Race during the 1950s. It was argued that freedom is indivisible in the sense that reduction of free speech in one area (in the theatre, say) affects production in others (in military science, say). But this seems not to have been the case in the USSR itself. After all, the USSR did not allow even its military scientists a general freedom of speech.

It seems, then, that a country can become or remain powerful whether or not it allows a general freedom of speech. The fact that Joe McCarthy's triumphs in Congress preceded Russia's triumph in sending the first ever man-made satellite into orbit around the Earth was probably a coincidence.

138

Wealth

Should freedom of thought be valued because it makes the nation rich?

Countries which encourage, or compel, their citizens to conform to the thought-patterns approved by government are not necessarily poorer than those which do not. In Japan and Korea, for example, the ordinary citizen is expected to agree with those in authority. School children are discouraged from asking questions in class and can even be punished for doing so. Yet these nations are among the richest in the world. It should be remembered, too, that there are several unfree nations which are so rich they can easily buy scientific information from the free world.

On the other hand certain kinds of freedom of expression can make *individuals* rich. It is said that the pornography industry, for example, has made huge fortunes for its entrepreneurs.

Happiness

Should freedom of thought be valued because it makes people happy?

This is partly the reason. If knowledge is hidden by government or people in authority (such as doctors, for instance) the individual's chance of making wise choices is reduced. Secrecy, lies and the suppression of truth all hamper the pursuit of happiness. It has been said that the function of speech itself is to rid us of irrational fears and that lies and secrecy are a perversion of this function.

Human Needs

Perhaps the main reason why liberty of thought and expression is and ought to be valued is that it answers an important human

139

need. An inability to speak out (for whatever reason) is a restriction or curtailment of the human capacity and the human need to *think*. When this capacity is curtailed by political forces human beings are reduced to a level lower than their best – the level of mindless conformity.

Knowledge and Truth

Another reason why free speech ought to be valued was proposed by the poet John Milton and the philosopher J. S. Mill. They believed that freedom of thought and expression increases knowledge and leads to truth. Thus Milton argues that religious freedom is a condition of religious knowledge and freedom of expression a condition of knowledge generally. Truth and knowledge are supremely valuable. Moreover (he says), truth will always defeat falsehood in a fair fight:

> Where there is much desire to learn there will of necessity be much arguing, much writing, many opinions; for opinion in good men is but knowledge in the making . . .
> Though all the winds of doctrine were let loose to play upon the earth, so Truth be in the field, we do injuriously, by licensing and prohibiting, to misdoubt her strength . . . whoever knew truth to get the worse, in a free and open encounter?

There are problems here. How are we to interpret the words 'free and open encounter'? Who is to decide when and whether an encounter is free and open? And what is to be done, exactly, when the encounter is manifestly not free and open? These questions bring us to the topics of defamation, racist literature and pornography.

Defamation

Should people be free to vilify one another in speech or writing? Ought there to be laws against defamation of character? Milton's words are not usually thought of as justifying libel. But what is libel? Can the truth be libellous?

The eighteenth-century jurist, Lord Mansfield, issued the following dictum:

The greater the truth the greater the libel.

Which is to say, truth can be more damaging to a man's character than mere falsehood. Now, British law distinguishes between criminal libel, seditious libel and libel as a tort, and Mansfield's dictum really has to do with criminal libel and seditious libel. But nowadays it is almost unknown for the State to prosecute anyone for criminal or seditious libel. Nowadays virtually all defamation cases in Britain are torts.

Libel cases in England are tried by juries and the juries have the responsibility of deciding on damages – which are sometimes colossal. When an ex-army officer sued the author Nicholas Tolstoy for libel, the judge, who seems not to have been much at ease with slang, unwisely told the jury not to inflict 'Mickey Mouse damages'. Apparently he thought 'Mickey Mouse' means 'foolish'. The jury then ordered Tolstoy to pay the ex-officer £1,000,000.

In England suits are rarely brought against big national newspapers because big newspapers are rich and can afford expensive defence lawyers and long trials. (In England it is not permitted to any lawyer, local or foreign, to offer a client a no win, no fee, deal.) On the other hand some wealthy men have managed to suppress unpleasant truths about themselves by threatening to sue. The late Robert Maxwell is a case in point. It is said that journalists in London had evidence that Maxwell was stealing money from his employees' pension fund yet no newspaper dared to print the information during his lifetime. After his death it was reported that Maxwell had effectively silenced the press by threatening to sue for defamation.

Some wealthy people always refuse to sue. There is a tradition, or rather a custom, which prevents the royal family from engaging in private law suits. This makes them a sitting target for scandal sheets. Readers of the British tabloid press are seriously addicted to scandal, especially sexual scandal, and the cheaper newspapers compete vigorously with one another to provide it. Mendacious attacks on prominent people are also used to promote the political opinions of proprietors and editors. Vilification of members of the royal family is a special skill developed by journalists working for Rupert Murdoch, a multi-millionaire newspaper proprietor who seems to have an obsessive desire to abolish the monarchy and establish a republic.

It seems, then, that the possibility of Milton's free and open encounter does not always obtain in Britain.

Mansfield's dictum was the rule in the American colonies as well as in England, and was maintained by some legalists even after the war of independence. Thus an American judge sitting in the state of New York in 1804 said:

Truth may be as dangerous to society as falsehood.

An attorney replied to this judge as follows:

Liberty of the press . . . consists of publishing with impunity, truth with good motives and for justifiable ends, whether it relates to men or to measures.

The author Mark Lane traces the legal principles upon which the First Amendment rests back to colonial days. In August 1735 (he writes) Andrew Hamilton defended a man called John Peter Zenger in a case brought by William Cosby, the colonial Governor of New York. Zenger had attacked Cosby in print and was arrested and imprisoned for seditious libel. The judge trying the case instructed the jury to accept the principle that truth is no defence against defamation, while Andrew Hamilton argued, on behalf of his client, that *men must be allowed to speak the truth*. The jury ignored the judge's instructions and found Zenger not guilty.

During the first years of the nineteenth century the basic law of libel in the USA came to depend on two principles: first, truth is the absolute test; and second, the jury, not the judge, must decide on whether libel has occurred. According to Lane American libel law was based for 200 years on the theory that the First Amendment does not protect writing (or speech) if it is both false and defamatory. He says:

> Elected officials, governmental institutions, large financial interests and all others could be tested, questioned, even vilified, so long as the allegations were truthful. The truth speaker was immune from prosecution.

Lane goes on to relate how these presumptions were eventually overruled. In 1964 the US Supreme Court unanimously struck down a case brought against *The New York Times* for defamation. The paper had published falsehoods about the plaintiff but the court ruled that falsehood, as well as truth, is protected by the First Amendment unless it can be shown that the untrue statements were motivated by actual malice. Since actual malice is hard to prove, libel cases against newspapers and the media have become comparatively rare in the United States. One unfortunate result is that the media are now free to speak falsely about truth-speaking dissidents.

Lane explains the ruling as follows:

> The metamorphosis of libel law in the US is a microcosm of the development of our nation – from early revolutionary commitment, a zeal to oppose and denounce royalty and tyranny, to abject surrender to business interests even when those concerns are inapposite to the interests of the nation . . . the courts, bowing to the industrialists who control the newspapers, television and radio networks and stations, have converted the First Amendment from a refuge for the truth speaker into a refuge for the liar.

If Lane is right it is doubtful whether Milton's free and open encounter between truth and falsehood always obtains in the USA today.

To give government the power to decide when encounters between truth and falsehood are free and open in matters relating to defamation would be dangerous. That does not mean that the courts could not be empowered, somehow, to rule in favour of truth.

Truth-speaking and Dissidence

Should truth-speakers always be protected? Do citizens always have a right to know the truth?

It will be useful here to draw three distinctions. First, we need to distinguish between honest folk and criminals; second, between public figures and private citizens; and third, between the public figures who rule over us, or aspire to do so, i.e., politicians and candidates for political office, and public figures who are famous but not especially powerful – for example, actors and musicians.

Citizens surely have a need and a genuine right to seek and, if possible, obtain information about the whereabouts and behaviour of particular criminals – con-men, thieves and fraudsters, for example. They also have a need and a genuine right to know about the behaviour, even (as Ross Perot says) the domestic behaviour, of their local and national rulers and would-be rulers. So people who speak truth about criminals and about politicians should be protected. But there is no real need to satisfy *all* feelings of curiosity about actors and actresses and musicians and so on, still less any need or right to pry into the behaviour of the ordinary honest folk who happen to be one's neighbours.

What about truth-speaking dissidents? In times of peace the truth-speaking political dissident must surely be protected unless we decide that freedom of expression is after all of little value. But in time of war, it has been argued, some truth-speaking dissidents might also be traitors. Yet if it is true, or even if it is false, minority opinion as such does not constitute treason. Ob-

144

jecting to a war, or to the way in which it is being waged, is not the same kind of thing as selling secrets to the enemy. In a democracy dissidents are rarely spies. Those who *are* spies and traitors can be dealt with under laws which do not attack freedom of speech as such.

Should dissidents also be permitted to say or write what the government or the experts regard as false? It is widely agreed that scientific and scholarly research will be seriously hampered if unpopular opinions are suppressed. Yet it is also said, and particularly by academics and scientists, that cranks and their cranky views have to be 'weeded out'. How this is to be done is a contentious matter but it is fairly obvious that, *contra* certain Marxist ideas, neither politicians, nor the so-called vanguard of the proletariat, are qualified to do the weeding.

Dissidence in politics and dissidence in science and scholarship are not invariably easy to separate since an individual can be a dissident in more than one way. Moreover, political questions and questions of scholarship (or even matters of science) can overlap. This is one reason why the dissident whose views are condemned by government or by experts ought not to be silenced, even by experts. If the weeding out is so strenuous as to silence him or her then it ought to be modified or abandoned.

Even when the dissidence is purely political it would be wrong to suppose that politicians, or the vanguard of the proletariat, are qualified to weed out views which happen to be unpopular. For no one is really qualified to weed out unpopular political opinions – which therefore ought not to be silenced unless, like racist propaganda, they persistently degrade human beings and/or lead to serious civil unrest.

Racism and Pornography

Britain's Race Relations Act of 1976 forbids employers to discriminate against members of minority groups. Individuals who believe they have been discriminated against on racial grounds can sue for damages. The Act also prevents the publication of racist propaganda because it contains a section which makes incitement to racial hatred a crime.

Britain also has a Sex Discrimination Act (1975) that contains somewhat similar provisions to the Race Relations Act with regard to employment. However, the Sex Discrimination Act is concerned only with torts and does not criminalize sexist propaganda or pornography. (A cynic might explain the difference by pointing out that there is not much money to be made by printing racist propaganda but big fortunes in pornography publishing.)

There is a considerable demand for commercial pornography, a demand that divides communities partly along sex lines. Many more men than women are attracted to porn. For most women, porn, especially the hard variety, is repulsive and frightening. According to evidence submitted by British Agony Aunts to the Williams Committee on Obscenity and Film Censorship (1977– 9), wives who discover that their husbands are purchasers of pornography usually feel disturbed and upset. The Agony Aunts and the committee itself agreed that most purchasers are men. Communities are also divided ideologically. Conservatives, religious people and radical feminists all believe that pornography degrades women and children – and men too. Much left-liberal opinion, on the other hand, though strongly opposed to racism, insists that censorship of pornography would be a violation of the citizen's right to freedom of thought and expression.

A common view among feminists is that pornography closely resembles racist propaganda. The one degrades black people and encourages white people to treat them badly in various ways, the other degrades women and children and encourages men to treat them badly in specific ways: humiliation, rape, child abuse, sex-murder. In other words, according to most feminists hard porn harms women and children and its production and sale ought to be banned or controlled.

Feminists define pornography as material which depicts and encourages violent and coercive sexual degradation. It represents in pictures or words the degradation of women and children through sexual violence and compulsion. It contains a powerfully presented suggestion that sexual violence and compulsion are acceptable forms of behaviour. Feminists compare it to advertising. Commercial advertising (they argue) degrades women by representing them as wholly concerned with trifling subjects like the virtues of soap powders and shampoos, but pornography is a far more sinister kind of degradation. It depicts women and children, not as full human beings, but as objects which men can treat in any way they like.

Left-liberal opinion is that even hard porn cannot be shown to be harmful. This view finds typical expression in the *Williams Report on Obscenity and Film Censorship*, published, in Cambridge, in abridged form, by Bernard Williams, the committee's chairman, in 1981. The Report (which ended up in Prime Minister Margaret Thatcher's waste-paper basket) has been largely overtaken by events. The committee wholly failed to predict the enormous growth in the production of videos and the resulting emergence of new avenues of pornography. Indeed the Report was out of date even at the time it was composed (1977–9) since it did not take any serious notice of the massive 'New Wave' feminist literature (1960–85) on the subject. In Williams's 1981 version of his Report there are 48 paragraphs concerned with research studies comprising crime statistics plus the conflicting views of psychologists. Fourteen of these 48 paragraphs are devoted to a demolition-job on the work of an anti-porn psychologist (a male). Objections from feminists, objections from Christians and Jews, and the 'tendency' of an undefined 'Women's Movement', are lumped together in a single paragraph (6.64) which ends as follows:

> the consensus of those parts of the Women's Movement from which we heard tended to attach greater importance to freedom of expression than the need to suppress pornography.

This conclusion is completely at odds with all mainstream feminist literature on the subject of pornography.

Nevertheless the arguments in the Report are worth looking at because they rely on quasi-philosophical reasonings which are still the mainstay of the left-liberal position.

The reasonings start from the premise that expression of opinion should only be banned (or controlled) if it can be shown to cause harm. The fact that only some types of 'opinion' are deliberately subjected to tests for harm was not a matter considered by Williams and his committee. Racism, for example, is not tested for harm, rather it is assumed to be harmful because of very weighty (though unanalysed) anecdotal and historical evidence. The Williams committee insisted that the sexism, if any, embodied in porn, should be subjected to psychological tests devised by experts. Although anecdotal and historical evidence was indeed submitted to the committee, for example by the police, in the end all such submissions were ignored. The expert psychologists, on the other hand, whose evidence was taken very seriously, disagreed among themselves. So the committee first decided that the case against porn is 'not proven', and then, by a slide, implied that it is harmless. A better judgement might have been that psychologists are not experts at all since experts in other sciences tend to agree on major issues.

Nowadays pornography (so I am given to understand) is easily available all over Europe and North and South America in the form of video cassettes. Much of it (so I am given to understand) is frighteningly sadistic. There is no sign in Williams's book that any member of the committee had actually asked to see examples of the material which feminists and the police wanted to ban.

It is wrong to suppose that all or even most commercially produced films and videos are expressions of free thought and opinion. The main thing protected, for the producer, is his capacity to make a lot of money. Porn videos are thus very similar to advertisements for soap or motor cars. The point of a soap advertisement is not to *express* an opinion, for who knows the advertiser's true opinion about the soap? The real point of advertising, and its real effect, is to influence behaviour by *instilling* opinions. The most effective advertisements do not baldly state that you would be well advised to buy this or that product, rather they suggest that you buy by telling little stories. One of the most powerful tools in the advertising business is the TV mini-story lasting 30–60 seconds.

Feminists and others argue that porn too instils opinions. It does not baldly state that men would be well advised to harm women, any more than the soap ads make bald statements about soap. Instead it instils opinions in the same way the soap ads do – by telling stories. The stories told in pornography suggest that the sadistic maltreatment of women and children is an acceptable and enjoyable form of behaviour. The suggestion is not made with mini-stories of 30–60 seconds but with moving pictures which can presumably last as long as a videotape.

Because the porn-sellers' products are closely similar in form to advertisements the claim that the products cannot and will not have similar effects (other things being equal) is quite implausible. But other things are not equal, of course, since sexual assault is illegal while buying and using a well-advertised brand of soap is not. So millions of people buy soap while comparatively few carry out sexual assaults. According to the Williams Report there were only (only) a few thousand sexual assaults every year in England and Wales during the 1970s.

Would people stop washing if soap were not advertised? Some would and some wouldn't. It seems only common sense to expect that, without soap ads to stimulate purchasing, washing would gradually become less common in the long run. Still, some extra clean people would go on washing come what may.

Would sexual assaults cease if hard pornography was somehow abolished? Again, it seems only common sense to expect that without the stimulation offered by pornography assaults would decrease. Still, some men would go on assaulting women and children come what may.

It is sometimes argued that watching pornography is a substitute for sexual assault. To my mind that is rather like saying that watching soap ads is a substitute for washing.

Left-liberals owe the world an explanation. They should try to explain why they believe that advertising soap increases sales enormously and also believe that advertising sadistic sexual practices has no effect.

CHAPTER THIRTEEN

The Right, the Left and the Green

'A Study of Economics as if People Mattered'

E. F. Schumacher, *Small is Beautiful*

Why Government?

In modern times virtually everyone is born and continues to exist under a government of some kind or other. People take it for granted that rulers and States are necessary for civilized existence and perhaps also take it for granted that government is mostly carried out for the good of those who are governed. Yet left-wing anarchists believe that States are merely instruments of repression and right-wing anarchists (libertarians) argue that the role of the State should be minimized.

The economist E. F. Schumacher wrote a book called *Small is Beautiful* and gave it the sub-title 'A Study of Economics as if People Mattered'. It would be good if governments always ruled 'as if people mattered' but history shows that such is not the case. History shows that government has too often acted as if Kings mattered, Chiefs mattered, Sultans mattered, Presidents mattered, Popes mattered, but not as if ordinary men, women and children mattered. In civilized countries – such as the USA, France and England – where the rule of law has obtained for decades or even centuries the law itself has too often differentiated between aristocrat and commoner, between slave and free, between Jew and Christian, and of course between men and women. Where there is no rule of law, or where the rule of law is not wholly effective, the lives of ordinary people might well count for nothing; whence such evils as slavery in the non-democratic countries of the Middle East, and the deliberate mutilation of children destined to become beggars in India (technically a democracy), and the custom, reported by V. S. Naipaul as still extant in the second part of this century, of West African chiefs celebrating their accession to power by bathing their feet in the blood of freshly killed human beings.

Do we need rulers and government? Would we be better off without them?

Since the eighteenth century many thinkers have agreed that the justification of government lies in the benefit of the people. Rulers are supposed to rule as if people mattered. Democratic procedures are supposed to ensure this outcome and in certain places actually do so, at least to some extent.

In the rest of this chapter I will examine three theories about the best way for governments to ensure the welfare of the citizens: first the theory of the free market; then democratic socialism; and then the views of the so-called Greens. The intention is to present a case for each theory in turn, using the works of three committed protagonists: Hayek, Bevan and Schumacher. All three authors place high value on the human individual and on human welfare and agree that without the rule of law no decent social system is possible. All see dangers in large, unelected bureaucracies. Their differences are not about ends or bedrock human values but about means.

The Theory of the Free Market

The theory of the free market is accepted nowadays by conservative governments everywhere. It also influences political parties which were formerly socialist in character – the British Labour Party, for example, and the Labour governments in Australia and

New Zealand. Free-market practices of a kind were adopted in Russia after the collapse of the USSR in 1989 and are accepted today even in communist China. The almost universal acceptance of free-market ideals might have something to do with the fact that the richer nations of the world insist that poorer countries can only expect trade and aid if they undergo reform, i.e., if they institute modern free-market economic programmes.

The theorists of the market sometimes call their ideology liberalism, or Reaganomics (after former President Reagan of the USA) or Thatcherism (after Margaret Thatcher, former Prime Minister of Great Britain). The theory stems partly from the works of Adam Smith (1723–90) and, more recently, from the teachings of the Austrian school of economics. Friedrich Hayek, who was born in Vienna in 1899 and settled in Britain in 1931, is one of the most influential members of the Austrian school.

Adam Smith wrote a famous book called *The Wealth of Nations* in which he penned the following famous words:

> Every individual . . . intends only his own gain, and he is, in this as in many other cases, led by an invisible hand to promote an end which was no part of his intention . . . By pursuing his own interests he frequently promotes that of the society more effectually than when he really intends to promote it.

Let us begin by explaining what the modern theory of the free market is *not*.

Current free-market liberalism is not directly concerned to bring about the social and moral reforms that English people associate with their Liberal Party and Americans think of as typical of liberalism. For example, it does not ask for 'soft' kinds of prison reform, nor for a ban on corporal punishment in schools; it is not particularly in favour of feminism, nor does it necessarily recommend the legalization of homosexual 'marriage'. Secondly, modern free-market liberalism is not quite the same thing as laissez-faire economics. One essential principle of free-market liberalism is that the State should actively create the right conditions for economic competition; it is unlikely that old-fashioned laissez-faire economists would wish to advocate that kind of government intervention.

Hayek lists conditions which he believes are needed for economic health. In the first place there must be a general framework of law, especially law which has to do with ownership and transfer of property. Next, government controls on poisons, and pollution, and working hours, are not always bad and might on occasion be necessary, for the invisible hand does not guarantee that private interest is invariably socially beneficial. Even State ownership of property is sometimes needed to produce necessities which are not of direct profit to owners and entrepreneurs – for example, roads and armies and technical education.

Free-market liberalism in general holds that liberty in economic affairs is absolutely necessary for personal and political freedom. Freedom is more important than democracy because democracy is a means, not an end. The fundamental basis of Hayek's thinking is a belief in the value of liberty and the value of individuals. He argues that those ideas, explicit in Christianity and implicit in the ideas of some pre-Christian thinkers, were not socially effective until commerce became prevalent in Europe. For many centuries individualism was stifled by hierarchical laws and customs which created closed shops in all trades and professions – including the profession of ruling. It was commerce, not politics or philosophy, which transformed the social systems of Europe, creating new and extremely flexible hierarchies everywhere.

How free is the free market? In *The Road to Serfdom* Hayek writes:

> It is essential in the first place that the parties in the market should be free to sell and buy at any price at which they can find a partner to the transaction and that anybody should be free to produce, sell and buy, anything that may be produced, or sold at all. There should be no price control and no restrictions on who may enter a trade.

154

However, a page or two later he says, in the small print as it were, that controlling production of poisonous substances and limiting working hours is not harmful provided the controls and limits apply to all businesses and not only to some. Somewhat surprisingly he also says

> There remains a wide and unquestioned field for state activity.

Socialist inefficiency

Much of the force of the marketeers' case comes from attacks on socialism. Hayek holds that socialist freedom is merely a demand that incomes be made equal. He adds the reminders that the word NAZI is short for National *Socialism* (in German) and that the dictator Mussolini, and the traitors Quisling and Laval, all began their political lives as Marxists. Socialism and democracy cannot be combined because socialism is a species of collectivism and collectivism need not have good ends and need not be democratic. Genuine freedom is impossible under socialism because socialism requires a planned economy and if you plan an economy you plan who will get what and who will work where so that the citizen loses control of his activities and his purposes in life. Finally, socialism is based on a false scientism. Human society has spontaneous forces which are unlike the forces discovered by the physical sciences. Socialism is based on the notion that a society can be engineered.

Socialist planning centralizes power. This is bad for two reasons. One reason is that centralized economic power is inefficient; the other, and more important consideration, is that centralization is not compatible with liberty.

Hayek claims that the Marxist belief that the free market has an inbuilt natural tendency to develop monopolies is a fallacy. He deduces this from the observation that most monopolies are fostered, even created, by governments. This observation seems to be correct: monopoly-producing tendencies of government

155

Ideology and Value

can be seen in Britain, America, Japan and many other countries. However, his deduction from the premise is itself fallacious since it is possible that goverments and the free market *both* create monopolies.

Free-market liberals hold that competition is the most efficient way of organizing things. Large firms are not more efficient than small ones, if they were they would not have to ask for government protection. When the State itself is responsible for production of goods and services it manifests all the drawbacks of a super-monopoly.

Why is centralized control inefficient? The reason is that it is impossible for a central agency to arrive at the synoptic views on which it is supposed to base its decisions. The decisions it reaches cannot be well informed because the facts needed are dispersed in a higgledy-piggledy fashion all over the country (or all over the world). This partly explains why centralized bureaucracies are notoriously slow. In the area of economics synoptic views are impossible and the free market is efficient partly because no one in the market aims at a synoptic view. Each buyer and seller looks at his own local situation, which he understands because understanding is possible at that level and because he has a motive (personal gain) for studying the available facts with care. Each businessman who is close to his local economic scene has a good understanding of that scene and can therefore make reasonably rapid decisions. The overall result is an increase in efficiency.

Liberty and bureaucracy

Free competition is the only method of economic organization which does not require state coercion. The more the State plans the more difficult planning becomes for the individual, but when control of the production of goods and services is diffused no one has complete power over anyone else. Hayek remarks that in a free-market economy even the poorest worker has more liberty than a well-off manager in communist Russia or fascist Italy. A millionaire in a free-market society has less power over his neighbour than a minor bureaucrat (a social worker, say, or a local-government housing officer) because the bureaucrat is backed by all the coercive power of the State. The more planning the State engages in the more bureaucrats will it employ and the greater will be the discretionary powers accruing to bureaucrats. Because massive quantities of planning are required by socialism the interpretation of the details cannot be decided by Parliament itself, hence many powers are delegated to experts and boards and trusts. This would not be a bad thing if the delegation consisted merely in the decentralization of the power to create general regulations for particular localities. But that is not what happens in a planned economy. What happens is that the people and groups to whom authority is delegated have to interpret the plans emanating from the centre. And that means they have to be given the power to make discretionary judgements in particular cases. Whenever and wherever discretionary powers are given to unelected bureaucrats the citizens develop a bitter sense of alienation and grievance.

Materialism and greed

Socialists believe that the free market encourages amoralism and a highly materialistic outlook. Greed is lauded by government, compassion and charity are seen as sentimental and useless. Marketeers reply that there is no reason why a businessman should not give money to charity and they can point to the enormous donations made to worthy causes by the great millionaires of nineteenth-century America. Moreover, according to free-market theory every increase in national wealth eventually filters down from the rich to the poor. It does not matter that wealth is ultimately the result of avarice because the final result is a continuing improvement in the well-being of citizens generally. Greed, if not morally good, is socially and economically beneficial.

Ideology and Value

At least one supporter of government planning agreed with the marketeers about the usefulness of greed. In 1930 the Cambridge economist, J. M. Keynes, wrote as follows:

> For another 100 years . . . we must pretend . . . that fair is foul and foul is fair; for foul is useful and fair is not. Avarice and usury and precaution must be our gods for a little longer still. For only they can lead us out of the tunnel of economic necessity into daylight.

By daylight he presumably meant universal wealth.

But foul is fair only in the comparatively short term. What of the long term? What happens when the 100 years is over? Keynes once remarked 'in the long term we are all dead' so perhaps he thought that worrying about the distant future is a waste of time.

Democratic Socialism

The economic system of capitalism has been attacked, and defended, by political thinkers ever since it first appeared. Marx considered that capitalism contains the seeds of its own destruction. Christians have argued that unrestrained capitalism is materialistic, selfish and unjust to the poor. Socialists of all types hold that it is inefficient as well as unfair.

Since there are several different varieties of socialism we must begin by saying what democratic socialism is *not*. Democratic socialism is obviously not National Socialism (Nazism, fascism) and it is not communism either. Communism adheres to the idea that capitalism can only be destroyed by revolution. It also holds that, although the State will eventually wither away, until it *has* withered away capitalism must be kept at bay by a one-party State ruled by a dictatorship of the proletariat. Communism notoriously fails to live up to its promises, thus in the USSR the sharing of profits from the nation's industries turned out to be an extremely haphazard affair, subject to much corruption by officials high and low. Privileged classes emerged (the KGB, the *nomenclatura*) whose members used the apparatus of government to coerce the unprivileged and to increase their own personal wealth. Here it is interesting to note that the principles of classical Marxism were developed when political democracy was in its infancy, i.e., when the State really was roughly as Marx described it – an instrument of class coercion. This fact not only underlies Marx's claim that revolution is a necessity but perhaps also explains communism's total failure to institute democratic procedures. (In a one-party State elections are, of course, a mere sham.) Under Russian and Chinese communism the State remained an instrument of oppression.

Democratic socialism insists that if capitalism is to be abandoned this must happen as the result of parliamentary elections. Under a democratic socialist government all the important decisions concerning the national economy would be made by the elected representatives of the people.

The central belief common to the different varieties of socialism is that all or most of the profits from the larger enterprises in agriculture and industry should be shared more or less equally between everyone in the nation. For this to happen the larger enterprises at least, and possibly all businesses and farms, should be run by the State. Marx thought that after some time had elapsed government ownership of property would cease to be needed and the State would wither away. But in the USSR the communist State did not disappear and it does not look like disappearing in China either. If the case of Russia is anything to go by it would seem that when a communist State does wither away it is replaced by civil war and crime and the harshest forms of laissez-faire capitalism.

Just as defenders of free-market politics base their case partly on the alleged weaknesses of socialism so socialists base their case partly on the alleged weaknesses of capitalism. It is interesting to note that each side accuses the other of gross inefficiency.

Ideology and Value

Injustice

According to Aneurin Bevan, the main thesis of democratic socialism is that poverty, great wealth, general education and democracy are incompatible. Sooner or later the educated poor will vote against politicians who protect the interests of wealthy capitalists – unless the wealthy first use their power and riches to destroy democracy. Human beings have probably never wanted total equality but they tend to resent inequalities which are capricious, or senseless, or based on criminality, or unsanctioned by tradition. Now, the inequalities produced by the marketplace are often visibly capricious and sometimes based on sharp practice or political favouritism. The feature lauded by free marketeers, namely, that the market makes room for anyone to rise in the hierarchy of wealth if he can, produces, in practice, much resentment among those who do not rise. The people left behind in the race refuse to accept that wealth is a sign of virtue or genuine success: riches, after all, can be inherited or got by bad means. The phenomenon of the *nouveau riche* is associated in many minds with arrogance and bad manners and senseless ostentation. New wealth is attributed (sometimes rightly) to mere luck (or worse). Resentment and feelings of alienation are not alleviated by the social dislocation caused by widespread unemployment. The American columnist Walter Lippman remarked that the ideal free market requires ideal workers, workers, that is, who are willing and able to move themselves around the country, with or without their families, whenever market forces make relocation profitable. Lord Tebbitt's famous advice to the unemployed, 'get on your bikes', is perhaps based on this perception: if so, it sounds like a good recipe for the dismemberment of traditional communities.

According to Aneurin Bevan the communist vote in Western Europe is not a vote for Stalinism but a protest vote against capitalism.

The most important question for a modern State is: How

should we spend the national economic surpluses which are created by work and technology? Capitalism cannot even ask this question since under capitalism there can be no method of deciding on priorities. Individuals and companies and trusts invest their own surpluses in whatever is judged most profitable for themselves. Democratic socialists believe that wealth is created by workers not owners or entrepreneurs. Entrepreneurs merely direct the workers in the production of wealth. This might be a necessary role but it is inaccurate to call it wealth-creation and unjust to reward it too highly.

Democratic socialists hold that a capitalist society will necessarily lack a decent order of values. The climate of the business world is amoral and exposes the psyche of the individual to unreasoning compulsions based partly on fear and partly on greed. These compulsions spread into Parliament itself. The political parties representing capitalist values allow retiring Ministers of State to profit in dishonourable ways from the confidential knowledge they gained while in office, while the smaller fry, the backbenchers, accept bribes from business lobbies and other dubious sources.

Instability

According to socialist thinkers capitalism is always unstable. Instability is caused by unemployment and by resentment about preventable poverty and visible greed. It is exacerbated by the depersonalizing process in which workers become parts not wholes, hands not people. Socialist thinkers claim that capitalism is also rendered unstable by a need for war.

Many valuable projects require collective action of a kind which yields no money profit. Fortunately not many of the people who work in preventive medicine or in refugee camps are motivated by thoughts of money. The huge improvement in the general health of citizens in the West is not the result of the profit motive but is due to the work of individuals (such as Lister,

Pasteur, Fleming, Curie, Roentgen) followed by collective (government) action. Bevan claims that free-market practices create dreadful anomalies in areas like human health. His words are perhaps vindicated by recent (1995) British news reports. It seems that the managers of private health insurance schemes have found that very profitable investments can be made in the arms industry. The Government has instructed the managers of National Health Service Trusts to go and do likewise, that is, to invest in whatever is most profitable. So some NHS Trusts are also putting money into companies which export arms. It is known that British companies manufacture anti-personnel mines and it is known that anti-personnel mines continue to cause many deaths and injuries long after the war they were used in is over. Most victims of anti-personnel mines are children in the Third World. Meanwhile, British volunteer surgeons and nurses are working in Africa and Asia trying to help the victims of British-made mines.

What can the market do if something necessary is not profitable? How can a free-market economy have an army, and technical education, and healthy workers, how can it afford to buy coal and foreign oil? The answer is that in such cases the marketeers usually call for government help – in the form of import–export regulations, or special subsidies, or, in extreme cases, war. The prudent use of scarce resources such as oil cannot be guaranteed in a free-market society because a free-market society has no means of deciding what is socially or nationally prudent.

Green Ideas

Green ideology receives its inspiration from several sources, two of the most significant being the writings of Gandhi and those of the economist E. F. Schumacher. The central ideas underlying Green values and the Green political agenda have to do with controlling expansion, denying the value of greed, protecting the

162

environment, getting rid of unemployment, and empowering poor people to live reasonably independent lives.

Expansion, avarice and the use of resources

The thesis that the perpetual expansion of industrial production cannot be possible on Earth, our large but finite Spaceship, might seem obvious or even self-evident. Yet all modern political parties, both in the West and elsewhere, proclaim the need for continual economic growth. Professor Walter Heller, former Chairman of the (American) President's Council of Economic Advisors (cited by Schumacher), said:

> I cannot conceive of a successful economy without growth.

The assumption that production can increase indefinitely is also to be seen whenever economists draw up graphs projecting production rates into the future.

Free marketeers and socialists alike know the difference between income and capital and know that capital must not be squandered, yet remain blind to the fact that natural resources, such as coal and oil, are types of natural capital which cannot be replaced. They do little or nothing to encourage the invention of industrial techniques which won't use up irreplaceable natural capital. The ideologies of expansion and 'wealth creation' recognize no ecological limits.

Gandhi wrote:

> Earth supplies enough for every man's need but not for every man's greed.

Green politics emphasizes the need to consider the long-term social and ecological outcomes of economic decisions and economic ideologies. Green thinkers argue that the avarice recommended by Keynes and others makes people stupid; greed and

163

intelligence are incompatible because intelligence in political and economic areas entails a capacity to take long-range views, whereas greed seeks benefits which are personal and therefore short-term. This view probably contains an element of exaggeration, yet also a grain of truth. The ideology of greed makes rulers pretty blind to facts even if those ruled can sometimes see the light.

Avarice explains why the richer nations behave so ruthlessly in pursuit of wealth. Being rich does not satisfy those who have been taught to think that foul is fair and greed is good, they wish to become richer and richer forever. It is because of this that the Utopia of universal wealth, which is impossible anyway, is made even more impossible by the consequences of expansionist economic theories.

However, it is probably fair to say that the average citzen in the USA or Japan does not know just how rich he is compared to people in the Third World. His mind is taken up with the material goods he sees all around him and which are advertised every few minutes on commercial TV. Aldous Huxley (cited by Schumacher) described the advertising of consumer goods as 'a pernicious form of adult education'.

The environment

Nowadays most reasonably educated people know that man is destroying the environment on which his life depends. Yet both marketeers and socialists continue to insist that industrial processes must be applied to farming, however bad the result. Agriculture deals with life and living things and cannot be successful in the long term if it ignores the need for health and replenishment. Different farming practices can make land beautiful or ugly, healthy or sick. The industrialization of agriculture rests on productivity without permanence and its techniques of mass production ignore 'luxuries' like beauty and the long-term health of rivers and soil. Small farmers, even if they adopt modern techniques, generally try to care for their land (because it is their capital), whereas big international firms can strip assets and invest the profits elsewhere. Current large-scale farming practices cause soil erosion, the silting-up of rivers, deforestation, destruction of useful insects and useful predators, and destruction of pollinators (bees). Industry and agriculture are polluting the Earth not only with ordinary rubbish but also with nuclear waste and with chemical and biochemical products whose long-term effects are as yet unknown.

Schumacher claims that marketeers and socialists alike take the line that the options suggested by Green thinkers – intermediate or small-scale technology, smaller political units, less psychological reliance on luxury – would be uneconomic. He remarks that the word *uneconomic* is regarded as a much more serious objection to policies than descriptions such as *immoral, corrupt, degrading*. Economic performance is every politician's obsession but what *is* economic performance? Processes are said to be uneconomic if they do not produce the most profit possible where profit simply means a money profit for those running the business/sale/production. Non-monetary benefits and benefits for society as a whole do not come into the matter because the ideology of endless expansion institutionalizes non-responsibility.

Perhaps some anti-Greens are capable (contra Schumacher's views) of taking small-scale personal action. Just as modern architects like to live in Georgian houses and never dwell in tower blocks so the owners of supermarkets probably don't buy their own food from supermarkets.

Mass production and unemployment

The development of more and more sophisticated machines causes long-term unemployment both in rich countries and in poor ones. The production of too many useful gadgets inevitably results in the production of useless people. Gandhi wrote that we should seek 'production by the masses rather than mass produc-

Ideology and Value

tion' because the result of mass production is that the lives lived by ordinary people are disrupted and rendered meaningless by poverty, by mindless work and by the alienation and social emptiness of unemployment.

The green alternative

Anti-Greens say that the only answer the Greens can offer is a return to a pre-technological age. This is a Gandhian solution but not one that Schumacher was looking for. Contemporary Green thinkers, like Schumacher himself, argue, rather, that technology should be directed to new aims. It should be used as if people mattered and as if the environment mattered. Technology is only destructive when it is harnessed to an ideology of perpetual expansion, and avarice, and gigantism in industry and agriculture.

Scientists and technicians should be trying to invent methods and equipment cheap enough to be accessible to poor nations and to most poor people. They should be devising machines which are suitable for small-scale operations and consistent with the dignity and creativity of human beings. They should be developing techniques that do not concentrate power and wealth in a few hands and do not turn working people into mere machine minders.

Anti-Green thinkers say that small economic units are not viable. Before the break-up of the USSR this used to be said about Latvia, Estonia and Lithuania, small places which were, and still are, richer than great big Russia. It was said about Slovakia and the Czech Republic before the break-up Czechoslovakia. It is still said about Scotland. Green thinkers reply that experience proves that small economic units and small States are more viable in the long run than larger ones. Small economic units are more viable because they preserve un-replaceable natural capital and, by sharing the workload, make it possible for most people to have regular employment. Small political units (small States) are more viable than large ones for roughly the same reasons. (Warfare, of course, brings in different considerations, though even in war a small State can sometimes defeat a larger one.)

The superior social strength of smaller political units is one of the lessons learnt from the collapse of the Soviet Union.

Finally, small nations that have been swallowed up by larger ones usually *want* separation and national independence.

Difficulties

I shall end by mentioning some difficulties and inconsistencies found in the three theories discussed.

Socialists and free marketeers try to answer political questions via economics. Now, many political questions have ethical implications, and answering ethical questions via economics is rather like attempting to answer scientific questions via biblical quotation. Politicians dimly realize, perhaps, that economics cannot answer social and moral questions, and the result is that many important moral and social matters are ignored by traditional political parties. Ethical questions about the environment, for example, tend to disappear from the political agenda.

The economic imperative accepted both by modern socialists and by marketeers means that democratic nations often feel forced to cooperate with nations which violate human rights.

In a highly managed society the citizen is not master of his social environment. Bevan acknowledged that bureaucracy limits freedom and acknowledged that socialism has not yet solved the problem of reconciling the socialists' need for bureaucrats and the citizens' desire for liberty, but believed that a solution will be found one day. Hayek did not predict that the politicians he inspired would reduce bureaucratic management in some areas (business, industrial safety) only to extend it enormously in others (health and education). For managers and bureaucrats are needed to create (and maintain) the conditions Hayek asked for, conditions which he claimed are needed to produce a free market. In the real world the British politicians who attempted to follow Hayek's principles ended up by introducing managerial trusts to run hospitals and universities and these trusts necessarily employ bureaucrats.

Government control of the lives of the citizens does not disappear under free-market arrangements. In the real world (in Britain for example) the free-market political agenda has created a large managerial class. Although managers are not invariably paid for out of taxation many of them work under government regulation. In this managerial society workers are disciplined by fear while employers and investors are inspired by thoughts of profit. Yet in times of high unemployment bureaucrats and managers too can lose their jobs, they too begin to be disciplined by fear. That leads to terrific feelings of betrayal. In short there seems to be an invisible hand at work which forces all politicians, including free marketeers, to extend the powers of the State.

What of the Greens? Well, some Greens, the Gandhians for instance, won't accept *any* technology beyond the spinning wheel. They can also be accused of political incompetence. Greens are good at inventing methods of direct action such as sailing into nuclear-testing grounds. They know how to gather in crowds when attempting to prevent the building of new motor-ways. They know how to harass whalers and politicians and meat exporters. But so far Germany is the only country where they have acquired any real political power. People attracted to more traditional political parties say that the Greens have no positive programme, no general programme. Others claim that to vote for a Green is to waste one's vote. To this last it can be replied that even the traditional parties started from small beginnings. As to positive programmes, the traditional parties change theirs continually; experience shows, therefore, that party political programmes appear and develop after elections as well as beforehand. Anyway, what the traditional parties actually do when in power is decided to some extent by pragmatic considerations rather than by promises made during election campaigns. Electors expect to be given positive promises on a wide range of issues, but since it can happen that the people they vote for will sooner or later break all but the most central promises this expectation is perhaps not very wise. The fact remains, though, that Greens tend to be one-issue parties and voters do not always find that very attractive.

Finally: some Greens worry so much about pollution that they begin to perceive human beings not as *polluters*, but as *pollutants*. Green politicians in rich countries with relatively small populations too often regard poor people living in more heavily populated places (e.g. Africans) and weak people (e.g. babies and the elderly) as *pollutants*. This attitude to the poor and the weak is seriously at odds with Schumacher's dictum that economic and political programmes should be devised as if people mattered.

Natural Rights as Justifying the Authority of the State

Natural rights are those which appertain to man in right of his existence. Of this kind are the intellectual rights, or rights of the mind, and also all those rights of acting as an individual for his own comfort and happiness, which are not injurious to the natural rights of others. Civil rights are those which appertain to man in right of his being a member of society. *Every civil right has for its foundation some natural right pre-existing in the individual* [my italics] . . . of this kind are all those which relate to security and protection.

Tom Paine (1737–1809)

(Tom Paine wrote his book *The Rights of Man* (1791) as a reply to Edmund Burke's *Reflections on the French Revolution.* Paine was born in Britain but served in the American army from 1776 to 1779.)

Either no member of the human race has real rights or else all have the same; he who votes against the rights of another, whatever his religion, colour or sex, thereby abjures his own.

Marie Jean de Caritat Condorcet (1743–94)

(Condorcet, a distinguished mathematician, made eloquent speeches on the popular side during the French revolution. But he was accused and condemned by the extremist party and died in prison.)

America:

We hold these truths to be self-evident, that all men are created equal, that they are endowed by their Creator with certain inalienable rights, that among these are Life, Liberty and the pursuit of Happiness. That to secure these rights, Governments are instituted among Men, deriving their just powers from the consent of the governed.

From *The American Declaration of Independence*

Congress shall make no law respecting the establishment of religion, or prohibiting the free exercise thereof; or abridging the freedom of speech or of the press or the right of the people to peacefully assemble, and to petition the government for a redress of grievances.

The First Amendment to the US Bill of Rights (1791)

France:

(i) The National Assembly recognizes and declares in the presence and under the auspices of the Supreme Being the following rights of man and of the citizen:

In respect of their rights men are born and remain free and equal. The only permissible basis for social distinctions is public utility.

The final end of every political institution is the preservation of the natural and imprescriptible rights of man. These rights are those of liberty, property, security, and resistance to oppression.

Natural Rights

The basis of all sovereignty lies, essentially, in the Nation [i.e. in the people]. No corporation nor individual may exercise any authority that is not expressly derived therefrom.

Liberty is the capacity to do anything that does no harm to others. Hence the only limitations on the individual's exercise of his natural rights are those which ensure the employment of those same rights to all other individuals. These limits can be established only by legislation.

The National Assembly of France: extract from the *Declaration of the Rights of Man and the Citizen* (1789)

(ii) The French people once again proclaims that all human beings without distinction of race, religion or belief, possess inalienable and sacred rights.

It solemnly reaffirms the Rights and Liberties of Man and the Citizen hallowed by the Declaration of Rights of 1789 . . .

From the *Preamble to the Constitution of the Fourth Republic* (1946)

(iii) The French people solemnly proclaims its attachment to the Rights of Man and the principles of national sovereignty as defined by the Declaration of 1789, reaffirmed . . . by the Preamble of the Constitution of 1946.

From the *Preamble to the Constitution of the Fifth Republic* (1958)

Canada:

WHEREAS Canada is founded upon principles that recognize the supremacy of God and the rule of law

The Canada Charter of Rights and Freedoms guarantees the rights and freedoms set out in it . . .

Everyone has the following fundamental freedoms: (a) freedom of conscience and religion (b) freedom of thought, belief, opinion and expression, including freedom of the press and other media of communication (c) freedom of peaceful assembly and (d) freedom of association.

From the *Canadian Charter of Rights and Freedoms*

The United Nations Organization:

Article 1: All human beings are born free and equal in dignity and rights. They are endowed with reason and conscience and should act towards one another in a spirit of brotherhood.

Article 2: Everyone is entitled to all the rights and freedoms set forth in the Declaration, without distinction of any kind, such as race, colour, sex, language or social origin, property, birth or other status . . .

Article 3: Everyone has a right to life, liberty and security of person.

Article 18: Everyone has a right to freedom of thought, conscience and religion . . .

Article 21: The will of the people shall be the basis of the authority of government . . .

Extracts from *The Universal Declaration on Human Rights* proclaimed by the General Assembly of the UNO on 10 Dec. 1948

The Controversy about Euthanasia: A Sample Case

I. Extracts from the *Northern Territory of Australia Rights of the Terminally Ill Act* (1995)

AN ACT

to confirm the right of a terminally ill person to request assistance from a medically qualified person to voluntarily terminate his or her life in a humane manner; to allow for such assistance to be given in certain circumstances without legal impediment to the person rendering the assistance; to provide procedural protection against the possibility of abuse of the rights recognized by this Act; and for related purposes.

Paragraph 3: Interpretation

In this Act, unless the contrary intention appears: 'assist' in relation to the death or proposed death of a patient, includes the prescribing of a substance, the preparation of a substance and the giving of a substance to the patient;

'certificate of request' means a certificate in or to the effect of the form in the Schedule that has been completed, signed and witnessed in accordance with this Act;

'health care provider' in relation to a patient includes a hospital, nursing home or other institution (including those responsible for its management) in which the patient is located for care or attention and any nurse or other person whose duties include . . . the care or medical treatment of the patient;

'illness' includes injury or degeneration of mental or physical faculties;

'terminal illness' . . . means an illness which in reasonable medical judgement will, in the normal course, without the application of extraordinary measures, or of treatment unacceptable to the patient, result in the death of the patient . . .

Paragraph 4: Request for assistance to voluntarily terminate life

A patient who in the course of a terminal illness is experiencing pain, suffering and/or distress to an extent unacceptable to the patient may request the patient's medical practitioner to assist the patient to terminate the patient's life . . .

Paragraph 5: Response of medical practitioner

A medical practitioner who receives a request . . . may assist the patient to terminate the patient's life in accordance with this Act or, for any reason and at any time, refuse to give that assistance.

Paragraph 9: Patient unable to sign request

If a patient who has requested his or her medical practitioner to assist the patient to end the patient's life is physically unable to sign the certificate of request, any person who has attained the age of 18 years, other than the medical practitioner[s], or a person who is likely to receive a financial benefit directly or indirectly as a result of the death of the patient, may at the patient's request

Euthanasia: A Sample Case

[and in the presence of medical witnesses and if need be an interpreter] . . . sign the certificate on the patient's behalf.

Paragraph 16: Construction of Act

An action taken in accordance with this Act . . . does not constitute an offence against the Criminal Code.

Assistance given in accordance with this Act by a medical practitioner . . . is taken to be medical treatment for the purposes of the law.

Paragraph 20: Immunities

A person shall not be subject to civil or criminal action *or professional disciplinary action* for anything done in good faith and without negligence under this Act. [my italics]

II. News Reports

AMA ASKS PM TO VETO EUTHANASIA
LEGISLATION (headline)

The Australian Medical Association has asked the [Australian Federal] Government to veto the Northern Territory's world-first voluntary euthanasia legislation before the cut-off date for a Federal override on December 16. In a letter to the Prime Minister the AMA's Northern Territory branch president, Dr Chris Wake, said the legislation 'violates, limits or abrogates' the ability of the Federal Government to protect life in Australia as it is required to do under the Constitution.

'This is extraordinary legislation and its ramifications in practice and in law are not clear' Dr Wake said.

The AMA believes the *Rights of the Terminally Ill Act* infringes

176

multiple areas of British and Australian constitutional law and that it is dangerous legislation because of these uncertainties.

'The more so because of the legislation's passage by a small and relatively isolated parliament' Dr Wake said.

'Accordingly the Governor-General [Bill Hayden] has a duty to refuse Royal Assent to this legislation . . .'

The Governor-General can disallow any Northern Territory legislation within six months of its assent . . .

Yesterday the Chief Minister of the Territory Mr Stone said he was staggered at Dr Wake's intervention. 'They will have a fight on their hands like never before if they seek to overturn any of our legislation' said Mr Stone.

Dr Wake said . . . that legal challenges could be based on Australia's international obligations under treaties governing the safety of life, and religious liberty, and also on constitutional grounds.

Dr Wake was supported by the President of the Northern Territory Right to Life Association Mr Tom Kelly.

(*The Australian*, 11 Dec. 1995)

The NT's euthanasia legislation has created 'naked fear' among Aboriginal women, raising fears for the future of everyday preventive healthcare programs in indigenous communities.

(*The Australian*, 6 June 1995)

ELDERS 'SCARED' BY NT DEATH LAWS (headline)

The Northern Territory euthanasia legislation has left many elderly Aboriginals too scared to visit hospitals . . . this legislation is regarded as culturally inappropriate [by Aboriginal people] . . . A bipartisan select committee of the Northern Territory parliament found there was widespread fear among Aboriginal people over euthanasia.

(*Canberra Times*, 10 June 1995)

Euthanasia: A Sample Case

Doctors who assisted Aboriginal patients to die if the NT euthanasia bill is passed could face traditional 'payback' punishment . . . Mr Michael Waljker, an aboriginal man from Milikapiti on Melville Island, said while consent for euthanasia might have been obtained from one family another part of the extended family could seek 'payback' against the doctor . . . the concept of choosing to end your own life is not accepted in Aboriginal communities.

(*Border Mail (Albury and Wodonga)*, 3 March 1995)

III. Extracts from a Speech in the Senate

There is no doubt that euthanasia is the easiest solution. Its very existence devalues the work and perhaps the funding of palliative carers. As Professor Lickiss, Director of Palliative Care at Sydney's Royal Prince Albert Hospital commented:

'. . . we can surely improve the care of our people without recourse to euthanasia, a violent solution which impoverishes the human – and medical – community. We have not, as a nation become so impoverished, nor as a profession have we gone so far astray.'

Contrast this approach with the callousness of the prominent advocate of pro-euthanasia, Dr Helga Kuhse. At a conference on the right to die she said:

'. . . if we can get people to accept the removal of all treatment and care – especially the removal of food and fluids – they will see what a painful way this is to die and then . . . in the patient's best interests, they will accept the lethal injection.'

Australia owes much to its multi-cultural heritage but it seems to me that euthanasia is a particularly white man's way of dealing with a problem. The Aboriginal Resource and Development service says:

'Dying is seen as something that should occur naturally, even for people who are terminally ill and any intervention by an outside person or agent should not happen, as it will immediately be seen as an act of murder or sorcery.' The Aboriginal community of Milingimbi wrote:

'We are nomads, hunters, food gatherers, ceremonial and cultural people who just want, and will give, comfort and tender loving care to our terminally ill relatives. Because our terminally ill relatives know that they are dying they usually always want songs to be sung, they want to hear the last sound of their traditional songs . . .'

(Senator Boswell speaking on 7 June 1995)

IV. The Slippery Slope Argument

If I accept that it is justifiable for a woman to kill her foetus in the womb because she considers her family complete or would rather have a child at a time that would better suit her career plans I know that I cannot continue to hold conventional views about the sanctity of human life at other times and in other states . . . parents should be permitted to kill small infants of one month old or younger.

(Peter Singer in the London *Spectator*, 16 Sept. 1995)

If Singer's reasoning leads us where we intuitively know that we don't wish to go (the dispatch of the unwanted) it is sensible for us to reject it. Singer rejects the sanctity of life because it is based on the religious belief of our 'being made in the image of God' and this he says is now part of 'a set of beliefs that most people have laid aside'.

Many humanists and atheists would argue that their conviction that human life has a unique and intrinsic value has less to do with religious sanctity than it has with their humanism. It was

179

people's humanity that was shocked when the gates of Auschwitz were opened as it is our human-ness that is revolted by 'ethnic cleansing' – that more recent example of dispatching the unwanted.

(Michael Jorgensen in the Melbourne *Age*, 26 Oct. 1995)

Glossary

'Agony Aunt' or 'Dorothy Dix': a press columnist who replies in a newspaper to readers who ask for advice on personal and domestic problems.

Alienation: A Marxist concept. Marx said that under capitalism workers are alienated [i.e., cut off] from the products of their labour.

Altruism: the theory that regard for others should motivate actions.

Capitalism: system in which private wealth is the basis for production and distribution of goods.

Communism: system in which public or State ownership of property is the basis for production and distribution of goods.

Consequentialism: theory that the rightness and wrongness of actions depends solely on their results or consequences.

Defamation: the two types are slander (which is spoken) and libel (which is written or depicted).

Deontology: ethical theory based on duty.

Egoism: theory or theories that self-interest either is or should be the basis of action.

181

Egotism: tendency to talk and think only about oneself; selfishness.

Embryo: offspring of animal before birth: unborn human offspring in the first eight weeks after conception.

Empiricism: philosophical theories which state that knowledge is derived from sense experience and introspection.

Epistemology: theory of knowledge.

Foetus: unborn animal offspring: unborn human offspring from the eighth week after conception up until birth.

Gamete: a single cell which unites with another in sexual reproduction. The product of the union of two gametes is a new single cell whose genetic code derives from that of the gametes.

'Greens': political activists or political parties dedicated to preserving the natural environment.

Hippocratic Oath: traditional oath taken in the past by doctors in which they promise not to harm their patients. It is named after the Greek physician Hippocrates (460–377 BC).

Humanism: the doctrine that human life and certain productions of the human mind, such as art and science, are intrinsically valuable and worthy of respect.

The word *humanism* has been kidnapped by atheists who treat it as equivalent in meaning to *atheism*.

Ideology: manner of thinking characteristic of a class or political party or of an individual.

Implantation: natural process occurring early in pregnancy in which the product of conception attaches itself to the lining of the womb.

KGB: Soviet secret police.

Glossary

Nomenclatura: Russian term referring to famous or important Soviet citizens 'naming' them as having special privileges granted by the State.

Occam's Razor: the dictum formulated by William of Occam (1300–48) which states 'do not multiply entities beyond necessity'.

Ontology: philosophical theories of existence/being.

Personalism: Christian doctrine that all human beings are human persons made in the image of God and thereby worthy of respect.

Personalismo: South American doctrine according to which political loyalty is owed not to parties or policies but to leaders.

Personism: the doctrine that, although healthy human beings in possession of memory and reason are persons and worthy of special respect, there are some human beings who are non-persons, or unpersons, and these are not worthy of special respect.

Pythagoreanism: philosophical doctrines named after Pythagoras, a Greek mathematician and philosopher who lived in the sixth century BC.

Rationalism: philosophical theories (associated with Descartes, Spinoza and Leibniz) according to which it is possible for the human mind to reach truth and knowledge by pure thought without recourse to empirical experience. Both Descartes and Leibniz were notable mathematicians.

The word *rationalism* has been kidnapped twice in modern times, first, by atheists and agnostics, who use the term to refer to their own views, and then, later, by some free-market economists, who use the word as a label for *their* views.

Reductivism: philosophical attitudes which offer explanations based on a few simple basic ideas.

183

Glossary

Relativism (1): 'Global': the theory that there is no such thing anywhere as objective truth.

Relativism (2): Cultural/Ethical: the theory that there is no such thing as objective moral truth.

Solipsism: ontological (or epistemological) doctrine according to which the only reality (or the only knowable reality) is a single isolated consciousness, for example, mine.

'Speciesism': a term of abuse labelling (and condemning) the opinion that human life is valuable and worthy of more respect than the lives of other animals. Speciesism, so-called, has been compared with racism and sexism.

Supererogation: a supererogatory action is a non-obligatory but praiseworthy deed which goes beyond the call of duty.

Tort: a non-criminal and non-contractual breach of legal duty leading to liability for damages; more loosely, a matter for a civil as against a criminal court case.

Utilitarianism: a theory or theories according to which the rightness and wrongness of actions or rules depends on how much pleasure and pain (or happiness and misery) they produce.

Zygote: single cell formed from the union of two gametes; the initial product of conception in animals.

Bibliography

This bibliography lists all the books and articles directly or indirectly referred to in the main text together with a few others for further reading.

Chapter 1: Morality and Humanity

Glover, J. *Causing Deaths and Saving Lives*. Harmondsworth: Penguin Books, 1977.
Singer, P. *Practical Ethics*. Cambridge: Cambridge University Press, 1979.

Chapter 2: Egoism, Relativism, Consequentialism

Dawkins, R. *The Selfish Gene*. Oxford: Oxford University Press, 1977.
Nagel, T. *The Possibility of Altruism*. Oxford: Clarendon Press, 1970.
Nietzsche, F. *Beyond Good and Evil* (trans. R. Hollingdale). Harmondsworth: Penguin Books, 1990.
Smart, J. J. C. and Williams, B. A. O. *Utilitarianism For and Against*. Cambridge: Cambridge University Press, 1973.

185

Bibliography

Chapter 3: Ethical Bedrock

Bentham, J. 'Anarchical Fallacies', in *The Complete Works of Jeremy Bentham*, vol. 2. Edinburgh, 1843; repr. in Jeremy Waldron (ed.), *Nonsense upon Stilts*. London: Methuen, 1983.

Kuhse, H. *The Sanctity of Life Doctrine in Medicine – A Critique*. Oxford: Clarendon Press, 1987.

Locke, J. *An Essay Concerning the True Original Extent and End of Civil Government*. London: Dent and Sons, 1924.

Chapter 4: Human Beings and Persons

Dworkin, R. *Life's Dominion: An Argument about Abortion, Euthanasia and Individual Freedom*. New York: Alfred Knopf, 1993.

Locke, J. *An Essay Concerning Human Understanding*, book 2 ch. 27; ed. Alexander Campbell Fraser. New York: Dover Books, 1959, by arrangement with Oxford University Press.

Locke, J. *An Essay Concerning the True Original Extent and End of Civil Government*. London: Dent and Sons, 1924.

Tooley, M. *A Defence of Abortion and Infanticide*. Oxford: Oxford University Press, 1983.

Chapter 5: Human Beings and the Other Animals

Diamond, C. 'Eating Meat and Eating People'. *Philosophy*, 53/206 (1978).

Lodwick, D. O. *Sacred Cows and Sacred Places: Origins and Survivals of Animal Homes in India*. Berkeley and London: University of California Press, 1981.

Midgley, M. *Animals and Why They Matter*. Harmondsworth: Penguin Books, 1983.

Rodd, R. *Ethics Biology and Animals*. Oxford: Oxford University Press, 1990.

Bibliography

Chapter 6: Human Beings and Machines

Mellor, D. H. 'How Much of the Mind is Like a Computer?', in his *Matters of Metaphysics*. Cambridge: Cambridge University Press, 1992.

Turing, A. 'Computers and Intelligence'. *Mind*, 59 (1950).

Wittgenstein, L. *Philosophical Investigations* (trans. G. E. M. Anscombe). Oxford: Blackwell, 1952.

Wittgenstein, L. *Zettel* (trans. G. E. M. Anscombe). Oxford: Blackwell, 1967.

Chapter 7: Euthanasia – For and Against

Brewer, C. 'Killing for Kindness or Killing for Convenience?' *British Medical Association New Review*, Jan. 1992.

Gilbert, J. 'Palliative Medicine'. *British Medical Bulletin*, 52/2 (1996).

Searle, J. F. Letter to *The Independent*, London, 18 March 1995.

Searle, J. F. 'Euthanasia and Intensive Care'. *British Medical Bulletin*, 52/2 (1996).

Chapter 8: Euthanasia – Logic and Practice

Foot, P. 'Euthanasia', in her *Virtues and Vices*. Oxford: Blackwell, 1978.

Glover, J, *Causing Deaths and Saving Lives*. Harmondsworth: Penguin Books, 1977.

Kingman, S. 'Lords Reject Legalisation of Euthanasia'. *British Medical Journal*, 308 (1994).

Pollard, B. 'Euthanasia in Holland'. *Quadrant* (Melbourne), Nov. 1992.

Van der Maas, P. J., van Delden, J. J., Pijnenborg, L. and Looman, C. W. 'Euthanasia and Other Medical Decisions Concerning the End of Life'. *The Lancet*, 1991 (cited by Pollard).

Bibliography

Chapter 9: Abortion

Braine, D. 'Why Abortion?' In *Light in the Darkness, Disabled Lives? Papers in Some Contemporary Medical Problems*. Collected by the Medical Committee, Order of Christian Unity. London: Unity, *c*.1981.

Dworkin, R. *Life's Dominion: An Argument about Abortion, Euthanasia and Individual Freedom*. New York: Alfred Knopf, 1993.

Feinberg, J. *The Problem of Abortion*. Belmont, Calif.: Wadsworth, 1973.

Gribbin, J. *In Search of the Double Helix*. London: Wildewood House, 1985.

Hamilton, W. S., Bayo, J. D. and Mossman, H. W. *Human Embryology* (revised 4th edn). Cambridge: Heffer and Sons, 1972.

Langman, J. *Medical Embryology* (3rd edn). Baltimore: Williams and Williams Co., 1995.

Tooley, M. *A Defence of Abortion and Infanticide*. Oxford: Oxford University Press, 1983.

Chapter 10: Professional Ethics

Chadwick, J. and Mann, W. N. (trans. and eds) *The Medical Works of Hippocrates*. Oxford: Blackwell, 1950.

Edelstein, L. *Hippocrates – the Oath*. Chicago: Ares Publishers Inc., 1979.

Haldane, J. B. S. 'Science and Ethics', in *The Inequality of Man and Other Essays*. London: Chatto and Windus, 1932.

Northern Territory Rights of the Terminally Ill Act. Government Printer of the Northern Territory, Darwin, Australia, 1995.

Wittgenstein, L. *Culture and Value* (trans. Peter Winch and ed. G. H. von Wright). Oxford: Blackwell, 1980.

Chapter 11: Feminism and Masculism

Aristotle *The Generation of Animals* (trans. A. Platt), in vol. I of *The Complete Works of Aristotle* (revised Oxford translation ed. Jonathan

Bibliography

Barnes). Oxford: Oxford University Press, 1981 and Princeton: Princeton University Press, 1984.

Aristotle *Politics* (trans. Benjamin Jowett), in vol. II of *The Complete Works of Aristotle* (revised Oxford translation ed. Jonathan Barnes), Oxford: Oxford University Press, 1981 and Princeton: Princeton University Press, 1984.

Dworkin, A. *Woman Hating*. New York: E. P. Dutton, 1974.

Freud, S. 'Femininity', in his *New Introductory Lectures*, in the collected edition of Freud's works (edited by James Strachey).

Freud, S. 'Female Sexuality', in *New Introductory Lectures*, ibid.

Haack, S. 'Knowledge and Propaganda: Reflections of an Old Feminist'. *Partisan Review*, fall 1993.

Huxley, J. Review of *The Dominant Sex* by Martha and Mathias Vaerting, in his *Essays in Popular Science*. New York: Alfred A. Knopf, 1927 (cited by Diana Long Hall, 'Biology, Sex Hormones and Sexism in the 1920s', in *Women and Philosophy*, eds Carol Gould and Marx Wartofsky. New York: G. P. Putnam's Sons, 1976).

McWilliams-Tulberg, R. *Women at Cambridge*. London: Victor Gollancz, 1975.

Schopenhauer, A. *Essays and Aphorisms* (trans. R. J. Hollingdale). Harmondsworth: Penguin Books, 1970.

Stanley-Holton, S. *Feminism and Democracy*. Cambridge: Cambridge University Press, 1986.

Wittgenstein, L. *Letters to Russell, Keynes and Moore* (ed. G. H. von Wright with assistance from B. F. McGuinness). Oxford: Blackwell, 1974.

Wollstonecraft, M. *Vindication of the Rights of Woman*. London, 1792. (Numerous editions are currently available.)

Tomalin, C. *Mary Wollstonecraft*. Harmondsworth: Penguin Books, 1978.

Chapter 12: Freedom of Thought and Expression

Dworkin, A. *Pornography: Men Possessing Women*. New York: G. P. Putnam, 1981.

Graves, R. *Wife to Mr Milton*. Harmondsworth: Penguin Books, 1942.

Bibliography

Lane, M. *Plausible Denial.* New York: Thunder's Mouth Press, 1991.

Milton, J. *Aeropagitica* (ed. K. M. Lea). Oxford: Oxford University Press, 1973.

Teichman, J. 'Freedom of Speech and the Public Platform'. *Journal of Applied Philosophy*, 11/1 (1994).

Williams, B. A. O. (ed.) *Obscenity and Film Censorship.* Cambridge: Cambridge University Press, 1981.

Chapter 13: The Right, the Left and the Green

Bevan, A. *In Place of Fear.* London: MacGibbon and Kee, 1952.

Gandhi, M. K. *An Autobiography.* Harmondsworth: Penguin Books, 1982.

Hayek, F. *The Road to Serfdom.* London: George Routledge and Sons, 1944.

Nozick, R. *Anarchy, State and Utopia.* New York: Basic Books, 1974.

Schumacher, E. F. *Small is Beautiful: A Study of Economics as if People Mattered.* London: Sphere Books, 1975.

190

Index

Index

Index

Printed in the United States
1187800004B/337-345